You Can't Make This Stuff Up!

FOSTER W. CLINE, M.D.

DEDICATION

Dedicated with love and humility to all those who have enriched my life so much: My wife, Hermie, and my children, Robin, Andy, and Winfield and their families. Special thanks to Jim and Charles Fay, Ph.D. and the wonderful staff at Love and Logic ® who have provided outstanding support over all these years.

ACKNOWLEDGEMENTS

I am so appreciative of my editors and proofreaders. I first impinged on my family and Andy Cline did a yeoman's job on first time through. Trisha Topham, a friend, and Kristen Corrects who were tremendous help with some of the editing. Of course, unending thanks to all those clients whose names have been changed and who enlightened me concerning the nature of the diverse, delightful, and exceptional human spirit.

TABLE OF CONTENTS

PROLOGUE

Throughout our lives, every one of us is blessed with opportunities to learn from others. Isaac Newton said it well, and his words have kept me humble: *"If I have seen further, it is by standing on the shoulders of giants."*

I learned from every one of the unique individuals you will meet in this little book. They provided a real wake-up call to surprising aspects of human nature—aspects that I was never introduced to in my training. They provided lessons that were at once shocking, enlightening, and touching. Over the years—believing that someday others might profitably learn from these folks—I kept a few notes in an old journal. In retirement, I came across this earlier writing. Re-reading some of my yellowed notes, I decided that yes—the young therapist of 50 years ago was right—these lessons of human behavior are worth passing on.

I have decided that if we are slow to learn from others, as was Peggy, a young woman you will meet later in this book, we'll get the same darn "Life Lesson" over and over again. The necessity of learning Life's Lesson is so central to our existence that God reminds us to pay attention to the lesson even as we sleep. Many of us have been visited by the dream in which we have enrolled for an important class, usually a college class, and, my gosh! We have completely forgotten to attend! Anxiously, in the dream, we learn there will soon be a test. The metaphor points to the lesson and cautions us to pay attention.

Those around us are our mentors for the lesson, which can only be learned if we are receptive and quiet and observe the choices of others. (We can be certain we are *not* learning when we're too busy talking ourselves.) We then have the choice to learn, approve, accept, or reject the lesson.

Let me give you an example. In the Spokane airport, two well-rounded ladies ahead of me were sliding their purses through the security machine. One, vibrating with indignation, said to the other in a most disgusted and rejecting way, "Jennifer is only fifteen and she's pregnant. I just don't accept it!" Her friend bobbed her head in agreement. One can't help but think, "Lady, you may not approve of Jen's behavior, but it's already happened!" She could choose to recognize reality, learn to cope with a situation she disapproves of, and become wiser in the process. Wise people don't confuse acceptance of a situation with approval of a situation.

Disapproval combined with a lack of acceptance almost always leads to a

i

lack of learning and certainly to a lack of wisdom. The lesson has been rejected, most likely to be offered again in another scenario down the line.

There is, however, an inner harp of acceptance waiting to play in all people. The mystics talked about that "harp unstrung." It sings in harmony with others when Life's Lesson is being learned. I think the harp sings when folks recognize the difference between acceptance and approval, between aggressive and assertive, between being self-centered and being centered on ourselves. As we greet and meet people along The Path, we must ever be aware of these nuanced differences.

For those who accept Life's Lessons, the opacity of being judgmental is replaced by the translucency of wry humor combined with acceptance. Can you see that soft little smile on the timeless face of Mona Lisa? I like to think her harp was singing just then because of something Leonardo said. Perhaps something of which she slightly disapproved, but she accepted it with a little smile. That smile of acceptance without approval grows to outright dark humor in very difficult dangerous or threatening situations: "Well, the great thing about this situation is that it can't get any worse!" The inner harp sings, "This is difficult, but I'm learning from it."

We see that wry humor expressed in individuals who are coping in prisons and in hospitals, in the trenches and in the emergency rooms. And along the way we all run into angry and often judgmental souls who ask, "How can you laugh about this!!?" Our answer must be that when we can laugh about a situation we are relaxed enough to cope with, learn from, and perhaps even perhaps fix the situation. Here is another story.

In our clinic, Sherry was an ever-relaxed and competent social worker. But not on one November morning! Her demeanor was a mask of tense anxiety. "Foster, I've got a situation, and I don't know how to handle it." This was, in itself, quite surprising, as Sherry coped well with almost anything that came her way.

I asked, "What's the situation, Sherry?"

"I'm seeing these *people*. They're in my room now. They're rigid and just can't speak to each other, and I just don't know how to handle it."

It was obvious to me that competent Sherry was allowing those folks to rub off on her. In our field, it's supposed to be the other way around. We are supposed to rub off on them! The contagion is supposed to flow in one direction only!

I asked again, "So, Sherry, what's the situation?"

"Jim is a CEO at a big corporation and I've been seeing him and his wife.

Today, they brought the babysitter to watch their kids, and it just came out that Jim has got the babysitter pregnant. Now they're all in my office sitting like statues."

"And you just left them sitting there?"

"I told them that I thought you might be free, and they thought it would be great if you could come in."

I'm thinking along the lines, "Good deal! This will certainly be a part of the lesson!"

When I entered I immediately saw that Sherry, of course, had given me a very accurate picture of the situation. These folks couldn't have been more rigidly motionless if they had been chiseled from marble. The babysitter had the eyes and expression of a deer caught in the headlights. The wife looked a bit like a huntress staring down the barrel of a long rifle with a bead between the deer's frightened round eyes. And the handsome CEO had the terrified expression of a driver who was about to hit the deer standing motionless in his headlights.

I was supposed to rub off on them, remember?

I ambled into the room, slouched into a chair, rocked it back, put my hands behind my head and said, "Sherry has explained this situation to me. This is just the old, old routine of the pregnant babysitter. So common, so common. You people never come up with anything new!"

And from deep within three souls, three inner harps twanged a single note of dawning acceptance. Three pairs of lips curled into wry little Mona Lisa smiles. Around three pairs of eyes, the rigidity of lack of acceptance melted a bit and three harps unstrung, preparing to harmonize.

As you read these short recollections, my hope is that you too smile with understanding, and your own inner harp resonates with stories that reflect your own life experiences—experiences filled with acceptance, humor, and wisdom.

1. SEX DRAMAS

We humans are really only *required* to manage four little life processes. We must sleep, drink, eat, and have sex. That's it. Four requirements for life. We can build a lot of excitement around just those four. Luckily for therapists, folks can have massive problems with them. Clients keep therapists busy with sleeplessness and sleep apnea, drunkenness, obesity and anorexia, and finally, of course, all sorts of interesting problems around sex.

Sitting in my office, Jane was totally pissed. She was tattling on Bob, who sat next to her, sulking. She explained, "After our swap night, I told Bob that I had really enjoyed sex with John. I thought that was what Bob wanted. At least that was what he always said. We were supposed to enjoy 'getting a little strange stuff,' he said. So I told him that sex with John was fabulous. But he went absolutely crazy! He picked up a chair and threw it against the wall! I wasn't even the one who pushed for the whole "let's swap and swing" plan in the first place! The whole thing was his idea!"

I looked at him inquiringly. "Bob?"

"Yeah, it was my idea. And Jane wasn't for couple switching in the beginning. But I didn't really think she'd *actually* enjoy it so much with John. And I guess…. Well, yeah, when she told me about how great it was, I lost it."

In one way or another, anger, disappointment, and jealousy over sex twisted like a red thread that sewed unhappiness through the lives of many couples that I worked with. Although sometimes, I have to admit, it was a struggle not to laugh. However, their situation wasn't very funny for the couples themselves. But someday, with the perspective of age, I'll bet they may feel like laughing too.

What could be more common than this:

Jake was unhappy. "Our sex life has just disappeared. There's no warmth in our bed. Jeannie is completely unresponsive."

Jeannie scowls at her hubby, "I'm not about to have sex with someone I don't even like right now."

Jake totally destroys his position by saying, "If we had sex, you'd like me better."

Jeannie throws up her hands. "Oh, my God! *Men!*"

1

One couple decided not to dissolve their marriage in a most unusual manner:

Theirs was not a happy marriage. In fact, Glen and Donna were about to break up. Donna was one of those people who agree, at their spouse's urging, to attempt marriage therapy. But for some people they really don't want it to help things work out. They want it simply to obtain a "get-out-of-marriage-free" card. Seeing a therapist was Glen's idea. Donna was there just to make sure marriage counseling didn't work! It's an old story…people popping into therapy simply to be able to say with conviction, "There! I told you therapy wouldn't help. I want out! I'm splitting."

Poor old Glen. He really wanted this marriage to work. Like so many, he actually wanted to hang around with a person who didn't want to live with him! That seems silly, doesn't it? But there are lots of folks like that. I could go into the reasons for it. But that could require another book. The point is, Glen was really heartbroken. And he was, all in all, a good man.

Donna had only one main reason for wanting out: Glen wasn't that good in bed. With more disdain than really necessary, she sighed, "He just doesn't turn me on." She was certain that Glen could only fumble around, not knowing how to satisfy a woman. She never considered that *her own* "on-button" could be the real problem and stuck in the off position. It's an old, old story. Lots of folks with intimacy problems blame their partner. They only really reach a screaming peak of unhappiness after discovering, when the divorce *they* wanted is finalized, that living with themselves is not really that enjoyable either. Worst of all, there is now no one else to blame. Of course, then the dissatisfied usually want back into the marriage. By that time, the other person has discovered how good it feels not to be hit on the head every day with a psychological hammer. Jumping back in with the previous partner is the last thing on their bucket list!

Donna impressed me as being that sort of person—a person unhappy in a marriage, serially blaming the other partner, and doomed to even more unhappiness if she was forced to live with herself.

According to Donna, Glen was a good father. He was a good provider. She had no complaints with the way he treated her. "Yeah," she admitted, "he's a good man." She even went so far as to agree that he was generous and loving. Even so, she made it abundantly clear in that first session with me that she definitely did not want to "hang around all my life with Glen."

I decided to see Glen alone. He needed to face the fact that, at this point, *nothing* could change Donna's mind. And he also needed to get a little perspective. He needed to come to understand that Donna's ditching him wasn't the end of the world. In fact, I assured him that with his personality, kindness, and well-paying job, he was likely to find a whole universe of women out there who would appreciate and love him.

To my surprise, Glen said he knew that.

I queried, "You know that there are other people who could love you?"

"Yeah, of course, but I want Donna."

Then he came clean and told me how he knew. He knew because he'd had a number of enjoyable extramarital affairs.

Sometimes secrets in a marriage drive people apart. Not that they always realize it. I asked Glen if he had ever considered telling Donna the truth about his dalliances.

"Heck no!"

Over the next 15 minutes, I made my pitch. "You know Glen, Donna wants out. Seriously OUT! The beautiful fact is, telling her the truth can't make your unhappy situation worse. And sometimes—rarely, I'll admit—the truth helps. When hidden things are out in the light, problems can be seen for the first time. Sometimes talking leads to working things through. Then occasionally, things really do improve. Besides, at this point, Glen, what have you got to lose by fessing up?"

With this approach, I was very slightly hopeful that their relationship might have something to work on. Perhaps they would at least talk. However, even in my wildest imaginings, I could never have realized how the truth would put a lock on this marriage!

Glen was understandably doubtful. "Maybe Donna *really* won't want me then."

"Hey, Glen," I asked him, "she *really* doesn't want you now, right? She couldn't want you any less?" Finally, with real trepidation, Glen decided to let it all hang out. And I called Donna back from the waiting room into the office.

"Donna," I said, "Glen has some things he wants to come clean about. Are you okay about hearing them?"

"Yeah, but it won't make any difference to me. Our marriage is over."

I said, "Go ahead, Glen."

Taking in a deep breath followed by a sigh that sounded like it issued from a dying black bear, Glen seemed to focus on some far speck on the wall.

Between a croak and a raspy whisper, he admitted, "I had an affair for two years with Nancy."

Donna was shocked into wide-eyed, stunned silence. Then she stammered, "Nancy! ...Nancy Engleman! My...best friend...Nancy?!! ...For two years! You.... You're kidding me.... You've got to be kidding!"

"No, Donna, it's true. But I had to break it off."

Still stammering and collecting her thoughts, Donna said, "*You* broke it off?"

"Nancy wanted to marry me!"

Donna is stunned. Absolutely and completely stunned. "...Nancy...Nancy wanted to marry you?"

"Yeah, but I turned her down."

At this moment in the office you could have heard a pin drop. But then, still hesitantly, Glen plowed ahead with number two. "I went with Dianna for 18 months. We went all the way...lots.... We liked each other a lot...."

"Dianna!" Donna interrupts. "Dianna Nelson?! You had an affair with her, too?!"

"Yeah, and she wanted me to get a divorce, but I wouldn't."

Donna says, with eyes like saucers, "Dianna...Dianna wanted to marry you?!"

"Yeah, she still does."

Then, as if he was a balloon giving its last little hiss of air before collapsing, Glen admitted, "I only went out with one other person. Honest. You know...Belle...Belle, who teaches Sunday school? I went out with her a little on some of the weekends...the ones that I said had to work...."

Donna, at this point, had slid from outright disbelieving curiosity into a stunned shock. "Belle.... Belle...not Belle.... So how did that go?!"

"We got along fine. But she wanted to leave her husband...I told her not to...'cause of the kids and all.... We don't see each other anymore, honest. Honest, Donna, that's it. I'm sorry, I really am."

Donna wasn't listening. She was very tightly locked into one inconceivable thought. "And they *all* wanted to marry you?"

Glen, still apologetic, quietly said, "Yeah.... I'm sorry, Donna."

"They *all* wanted to marry you?!"

In the next few moments, it was obvious to me that Donna knew all these women well. From her stunned silence it was apparent that she was struggling with a cauldron of hot emotions. Shock, anger, and even jealousy. I received the strong vibes that, as much as she might hate to admit it, she had been friends with these women and had respected them. And all three thought her husband was a catch! This was not only disconcerting, it was a massive wake-up call. If fireworks didn't explode in their bedroom, it *might not be Glen's problem!*

Donna looked at her husband with obvious anger somehow mixed with the dawning of a strange new respect. To my own utter shock, Donna ordered, with an angry little spark in her eyes, "Well they can't have you. I'll tell you that!"

And they stayed married!

I'd like to tell you that they stayed happily married ever after. But I just don't know for sure. I do know that during the weeks I worked with them, Donna brought up memories that would lead anyone to discount the joy of sex with any man. She remembered painful childhood experiences with her dad. And once Donna started to unfold her wings of self-awareness, it changed her responsiveness to Glen and he was inclined to keep his package exclusively reserved for his wife.

2. THE FUTILITY OF OVERINVOLVEMENT

God has a plan, right? It's calming to believe that He really does have a plan. When a catastrophe occurs, it's not really that bad. Because it's just a part of His old hidden plan. When things go *really* badly, it's still okay in the long run, 'cause "everything works together for the good," right? Things only *appear* horrible. When we pray for a life that is flickering and about to flutter out, God, always on duty, listens and answers our prayers. But we're told that like all good parents, he tends to say "no" quite a bit. Of course, when things go well, it shows the power of prayer. When lots of people all pray together, we're told that helps. All Christians know God is a lot less likely to say "no" when a whole bunch of folks are praying for the same result.

Darn it, I didn't really pray for Bobby. But lots of other folks did. Peggy, his mother, was a church regular and she and the ladies of her church ran a prayer chain that slithered like a snake through the town of Kirkland, Washington. In retrospect, I wish I had prayed too. I'll admit it. But, in my own defense, I was completely blind to the possibility that Bobby would *actually die*. I just didn't even *imagine* that it would happen. This lack of concern on my part was unconscious. I wasn't even aware of my lack of concern! Therapists do have an unconscious of their own. And the way it works is as tricky for us as it is for you. I no more thought about Bobby's death than I think about the hair on my back. It just was there, that nasty possibility that he would die, but not up front in awareness. That's just the way most of us handle the really bad stuff.

I met seven-year-old Bobby while in training at the University of Washington Child Outpatient Clinic. Bobby was going to have surgery, and I was assigned to prepare him for it. Jack Townsend, the surgeon, was technically great. He was well respected, and when someone was laid out on Jack's table, it was expected that they would always recover from the knife. So, this kid wasn't going to die in surgery.

That idea of his spark flickering out was buried so deep in my cortex that I, myself, would have needed therapy to find it! Later, in an article I published in the *Journal of Child Psychiatry* with Dr. Michael Rothenberg, we reviewed my therapy with Bobby. In it we tried to shed a little light on why I was so surprised by his death. Even before the days of multimillion-dollar malpractice awards, we physicians, maybe more than most, didn't cotton much to surprises. In preparing for the article, we came up with the probable explanation. The explanation made sense in the article, and in re-reading those old yellowed pages, I still believe it. You see, Andy, my oldest son, was just seven years old at the time. Little Andy was the same age as Bobby. Both Bobby and Andy were handsome little brown-eyed towheads. If I had been able to foresee that rickety old man death might clamp his bony fingers around Bobby, it might have awakened me to the truth that the sneaky old coot could very well creep over to our house and grab Andy, too. We just can't take smooth times for granted, can we? If you think too much about the bad stuff, you can get downright preoccupied.

Jack Townsend was a forward-looking, holistic cardiac surgeon, so after scheduling Bobby for the cardiac operation, he had referred the child to us so that we might help prepare him psychologically for this second and very difficult mitral valve repair. Townsend firmly believed that attitude made a difference in surgical outcome. Mitral valve repairs can be dicey at times. This was a second operation, and fibrous tissue from the first is tough, slow to heal, and makes the operation more difficult.

So I started seeing Bobby. He was a perpetually sunny, alive little kid, with an energetic dreidel spinning inside him. I could not imagine that dreidel slowing, wobbling, and skidding to a stop....

But that's just what happened. He was rolled into the operating room and never woke up. Died right there on the table, with IVs sticking out of every extremity. He died looking like a pincushion, just the way he, himself, in play therapy had predicted his end. He had worked with the little clay man, operating on it while playing doctor. He had diligently bent over his little clay patient while wearing a paper towel pretend mask over his nose and mouth. The little clay figure was often full of punched holes where Bobbie had shoved in shots and sliced in pretend IV tubes. Cuts had been carefully made with his plastic knife. A round glob of red clay was the pretend heart. One day in our session, he took the glob out, stitched it up with a paper clip needle and then mashed it back into the cavity in the little green chest. It didn't stick in there very well, and that day, with a rare resignation that shuddered up from his depths, he anxiously said, "Well, this is too hard to fix, all the scarring from his other operation is just too tough to cut through. I guess we'll just have to let him die." To me, that came out of the blue. I had never discussed scar tissue at all. We hadn't discussed the truth that the second operation would be more difficult. His statement utterly surprised me. In fact, I was low-grade horrified. But honest to God, I still didn't consciously believe this little trooper could actually be predicting his outcome.

"Oh, no, doctor," says I, recorded forever on the fuzzy old black-and-white video of that session, "We won't let that happen.... Surely, we can do something." Viewing that tape, I realized later I was definitely an overly-optimistic assistant in that predictive operation. But even now, I think the child needed that hopeful comment, for he brightened and said, "Sure, we can do something." In the article written later, Dr. Rothenberg and I wondered if I might not have explored his feelings of death or the hereafter at that point. But we both agreed that probably the way I handled it was best.

Bobbie responded by sewing up the clay heart and squeezing it back in the clay chest. It looked okay that memorable afternoon, but it inadvertently came apart when we moved the clay figure off the "operating table" where he had placed it. And that perfectly predicted his future.

Later, when reviewing the unsuccessful operation, the surgeons came to the conclusion that Bobby's cardiac sutures blew out shortly after surgery, about the time he was being lifted from table to gurney, heading to a recovery room that would never be used.

Bobby's mom, Peggy, was an interesting lady. Tough. Troubled, but tough. Not just troubled over Bobbie. There were other things. She had lived a hard life growing up as an Army brat, the daughter of a first sergeant who commanded everyone in the family like enlisted troops. She had seriously hated her dad. Angry and resentful, she fled the family at 15 and promptly hopped into bed with Larry, got pregnant, and married him. Larry was a controlling and demanding chief Navy engineer. Isn't that the way these things go? Peggy married the father she hated. I only met the guy once, at Bobby's funeral. He impressed me as oily, bordering on slimy. From what Peggy said, he had trouble with all women, but then I only had her point of view. Her favorite expression was, "Larry treated me like dirt." When Peggy was pregnant with Bobby, their only child, Larry encouraged her to have an abortion by kicking her swollen stomach during a fit of abuse. It almost worked, but after a lot of bleeding, Peggy kept the child. However, she always blamed Larry for Bobby's congenital cardiac defect. And who knows?

When you go through a child's death with another person, especially a parent, you become bonded somehow. Bobby's passing was a loss to us both, but certainly more to her than to me. Even so, it was almost impossible not to empathize—almost to the point of falling into the bottomless well of Peggy's sorrow. Bobby was her only child, and she was then divorced and didn't date. She had been totally absorbed in her son's medical problems. Bobby and his illness were all she had. The anguish Peggy felt after his death struggled its way up from black depths that most people would rather not know about. I have to say, all her parenting energy had worked wonders because Bobby was a real winner of a little kid. He was one of those kids you just can't help but love.

But back to the point: Any heavy trip that two people go though together leads them to walk a little closer though life. For a while, at least, I allowed myself to become slightly over-involved in Peggy's life.

Peggy had married (and divorced) young. And at the time of the death of her seven year old, she was in her late 20s. She was good looking— actually classy—although her countenance might have been a tad chiseled, almost hard. But then, her life had been hard.

Peggy was the first to admit that she had always "batted zero" with men. First her dad was an A-1 loser, then she married Larry, who beat her up physically and psychologically. Now her only son had up and died. In her misery, she saw no good way out. She made an observation shared commonly by a lot of unhappy single women in those days when couples married younger: "*If* there is a good man out there, he's married. If he's a really good man, he won't leave his wife because of an affair with me. If he's my age and not married, it's because he has intimacy and commitment problems or is loser and women have already dumped him. So whether I go out with a married or unmarried man, I lose."

Hopelessness peeked out of her depression, as it almost always does. And in reality, there could be a smidgen of truth to her sad observation. It did appear to me, during my years of practice, that there were many more available quality single women in their middle years than there were good men of the same age.

So there I was, helping pretty young Peggy through nearly inconsolable grief when Tom walked through the front door of the clinic. Tom was tall, dark, and handsome. I'm serious. He was athletic and healthy, a young businessman, a CEO of his own company. He was your basic winner. He wanted some counseling, he said, to help him through a grief reaction. He had heard of me, and was willing to wait for an appointment. Tom had two beautiful boys, seven and nine. After his wife's death, he had analyzed his depression, was able to cope with his loss, and knew it would get better with God and time, but still felt it would help if he could "talk things through" with someone who had been around the bend with many others who had walked beside the man with the sickle. Helen, Tom's wife, had suffered a protected and painful death before succumbing to cancer. They had a loving eleven-year relationship, and now he missed her terribly.

I saw Tom over several months. Before I met him, during the time that he had nursed his dying wife, the two of them had lovingly, with courage, faced death together. They had discussed Tom's options for handling life subsequent to her passing. Tom stumbled though the stages of loss rapidly, partly having done some of that painful work with his wonderful wife while he cradled her during the final months of their loving relationship. Because of their good communication and love, Tom had worked through

9

denial, anger, and bargaining before I even met him. But he could still use some help with acceptance and wanted to bounce off ideas for the future with someone he could trust. It didn't take a therapeutic wizard to recognize that this was a solid man who had looked right into the empty orbits in the skull of the man with sickle and had not flinched. He had borne his pain, and was ready to explore his options. His boys were terrific, and it became increasingly obvious to me that this nice man was a solid, caring, and responsible father. His two young boys were handling the situation as well as could be expected and were even continuing to do well in school while coping with their mother's passing. And, most hopefully for Tom's future, he had experienced a happy marriage until cancer had wormed its nasty way into ending his life with his wife. Certainly this man had no hint of problems with women.

At about this time, Peggy was glancing doubtfully but hopefully out of her cocoon of grief and looked like she might be ready to unfold her wings a bit, too. I was seeing both these people on a weekly basis, and I couldn't help but think....

...The kind of thinking that can shove a therapist to stretch the accepted bounds of professional ethics.

Could I be helpful to both of these people by somehow connecting them? I couldn't seem to keep from peeking past the great professional dictum: *Don't get involved in the personal lives of your patients.*

These were two nice people. Pretty Peggy had a few issues, of course, but handsome Tom was a definite unmitigated winner and would be *so good* for her. "Cripes," I thought, "she deserves a nice guy for a change, doesn't she?" The whole situation was filled with options that just couldn't be fulfilled by simple counseling. Here was a beautiful young woman who had lost a seven-year-old son. Here was a handsome, thoughtful young man with two beautiful boys, seven and nine, who had lost their mother.

Why, it would almost be unethical *not* to arrange a meeting, right?

I had some finesse. It's not like I just waded right in. I was tactful, talking with Peggy first. I told her that I was seeing a young man with a couple of very nice boys, the youngest of whom was just the age that Bobbie would have been. The man's wife had died. He and his wife had experienced a wonderful relationship. Would she be interested in meeting him?

"Don't you set me up to meet some turkey," was Peggy's quick response. "I've had enough turkey men in my life."

I had an equally quick response, "Hey, Peggy. I'm a super shrink. And this guy has my certified seal of approval. Do I look like the type that would set

10

you up with a turkey?!" So, Peggy agreed to my giving Tom her name and telephone number. I promptly did that on the following Thursday. He immediately looked forward to calling her on the phone and taking her out to dinner. He wanted to take her someplace really nice.

Okay, I'll admit it. I had voyeuristic anticipation. I imagined the fun they would have getting together, talking about their boys. I could just see empathetic Tom being so compassionate and understanding about Bobby's death. They had so much in common and so much to share. During the week preceding their Saturday night date, thoughts about their meeting crept unbidden into my brain when I was also devoting my attention to other things. But, hey, I could multitask.

I won't say I went so far as wondering what I would *wear* as their best man at the wedding. And I wasn't into pushing the exact chapel where the wedding would take place. But certainly there were a number of beautiful little chapels around outside the city that they might use. Perhaps I should talk to them about that, too. Off the clock, of course. I wondered how many kids they might cook up together. Children of their own. They'd probably produce great kids—Bobby was. Tom's kids were certainly winners. Of course they were about due for a girl, weren't they? So these were the thoughts that were kicking around my synapses when Peggy returned for her first session after their date.

She was a little too quiet after sitting down. I half expected her to be more bouncy. "How'd it go with Tom?" Had something had gone wrong? If so, what in the world could it have been?

"Oh, him," Peggy said dismissively. "First of all, he came with a bouquet of flowers and he didn't even know me! And then, he was always opening doors for me. I can open my own doors! You know how I feel about chauvinistic men. And then over dinner, Foster, I couldn't even get a good discussion going with him."

"What do you mean by 'discussion'?"

"You know, Foster, a good give and take. Something *lively.* People can't agree on everything."

Suddenly I realized that by *lively,* this lady meant that she wanted to dredge up something to *fight* about. As she talked, I realized that Tom was a damn sight too *nice.* Poor Peggy. Like a character in one of Shakespeare's plays, Peggy had scripted her role to interact only with demanding, controlling, and difficult men. Someone who would bring flowers and open doors, someone who wouldn't even fight about something in a first dinner conversation just didn't have the necessary qualities to be a partner for

11

Peggy. Peggy said she found Tom *boring.*

All this was grist for the mill, and we worked together to help her gain insights from this experience. And I'm sure she did. But Peggy and Tom never had another date. That was probably a good option *for him,* at any rate. The compatibility just wasn't there. Their personalities just didn't fit. In the years following my experience with Peggy, I counseled many other women who had suffered difficult relationships with their fathers.

I leaned that they generally used a common word for nice guys. They are *boring!*

3. DIAGNOSIS BY HOUSEKEEPING

Emma Alseron was an enigma. Her problem stumped everyone. By the time I became involved with her, she'd been on sixth floor, medical unit, for about a month. The clinicians there had run about every test they could on her and for certain she was not improving. It looked as if Emma was eventually going to disappear in a pool of her own pus.

Her illness was bizarre. When she'd first been examined in the emergency room at King County Hospital, there had been only that one oozing blister on her left thigh. It looked like a badly infected insect bite where the bug toxin, gone wild, was eating away at an ever-increasing circle of red-black dead and dying tissue.

Emma reported that before coming in she had been out working in her garden, grubbing around in dirt and manure all morning. Then, that very afternoon, this sore appeared. She said she thought she had been bitten by an insect when she was sitting and planting. She wasn't too worried at first, but then the blister began to grow and ooze pink fluid. She became increasingly concerned as the sore marched right ahead from the size of a dime, to a penny, to a nickel and then to an angry inflamed quarter. Over the past few hours before she drove herself into the ER at King County Hospital, it had been growing deeper and uglier. "Do you think it could eat my whole leg away?" Emma appeared to be a brave lady, but her lip quivered a little and she grimaced when she pulled off the yellow-red 4x4 bandage covering the mushrooming ulcerous sore that was continuing to fester and dig away in its red crater. With little concern, the physician saw the few angry red threads of inflammation snaking up toward the groin anxious to do battle with the awaiting lymph nodes. Sometimes this is indicative of a local problem that really wants to reach out and wreak havoc throughout the whole body.

In the ER a scraping of the angry edges was sent to pathology for microscopic examination. After about an hour, a puzzling answer came back. The wound showed severe necrosis and eosinophilia but no bacteria. (The finding meant that there were a lot of dead skin cells and white cells were valiantly fighting some unknown infection. Eosinphils are the type of white cell that may also indicate allergy.) This was not a happy finding but it was not specific either. It meant that whatever attacked Emma was definitely eating away at her skin and causing the white cells to rush forth in what appeared to be a tough battle to contain the unknown problem.

The physician on call in the ER didn't know for certain how to handle the

13

problem. He gave the usual advice that docs give when they are uncertain: "Watch it. Cover it with a topical antiseptic ointment and come back tomorrow if it's worse." Thankfully, God seems able to handle most problems. Watched problems do generally disappear. If they don't improve, harm is usually not increased by observing things for a day.

Emma was then given an appointment to the dermatology clinic on the following day. She was also provided with the antibiotic/cortisone ointment to smear on the spot in hopes that this would help. Emma was minimally mollified. "My mother died of cancer. All my life I've been afraid of cancer. Could that be what it is, doctor?"

She was assured that there was no apparent sign of cancer.

But the examining physician was worried, and ended his chart note: "This slightly obese, pleasant woman denies allergies, physical trauma, or past history of epidermal lesions. This is a puzzling lesion. Diagnosis is uncertain, r/o (rule out) staph or fungal infection, collagen or other autoimmune disease. Appointment made for return to dermatology clinic tomorrow."

On the following day an even more worried Emma appeared in the dermatology clinic with a new and growing angry red blister on her opposite calf. It too was starting to ooze. The original thigh burn, or whatever the heck it was, continued to weep, apparently thriving, ointment or no.

The dermatologist, in addition to sending a new specimen to the pathology lab, examined the ooze from the new lesion in the clinic and again saw that the white cells were obviously gathering and continuing to put up a valiant fight, but there was nothing that would specifically identify the cause of the problem. An old remedy that can be helpful was prescribed, a tar based ointment with a powerful anti-inflammatory in combo with one of the newer antibiotics. Emma, now definitely fearful, was told to return the next day. Her quivering concern about the competency of the obviously puzzled physicians was apparent.

Upon her return the next day, a small but worrisome crater in the center of her abdomen had appeared. Whatever nasties were feeding off Emma, they evidently were not confining themselves to the extremities and now could be bloodborne. Emma insisted that she was using no new soap or perfume and that her clothes were the same as she had always worn. Whatever was eating away at her certainly meant business, regardless of tar, anti-inflammatory and steroid topical medication. Now a very slight low-grade fever was raising its ugly head. The circumference of the two original sores had expanded and the centers looked deeper and angrier. No more messing

14

around with this! Emma was admitted to the hospital in the hopes that a complete work-up and interdisciplinary consultations might help.

After a diagnostic week in the hospital, Emma continued to baffle the best clinicians. Her lesions would start to heal and then erupt in a brand new outbreak. After ten days in the hospital, a psychiatric consultation was requested. That's how I became involved. I was on the psych-medical rotation.

I approached the internal medicine doc that had requested our consultation.

"What's up, Ted?"

After he told me the story as I have reported it here, I asked, "Gees, Ted. Interesting. But why a psych consult?"

"You know, nothing I can put my finger on, but…. Cripes, I don't know. It's a gut feeling about this lady. There's probably nothing there, but will you just take a look-see?"

I saw Emma. She sat in bed with a chronically congenial smile. She was friendly but perturbed about her situation. That was certainly understandable. Emma lived alone with three cats. She worked part time as a waitress. She didn't particularly like the job and had bounced from café to café, usually changing jobs after about three months of employment. I made a note to check employers about her performance. She gave a lot of excuses why they couldn't be reached, or the restaurants had changed hands, and various and sundry other reasons why it would be difficult for me to check. It made me low-grade suspicious and I felt she was probably not being completely open with me. Perhaps she was hiding something, but I certainly had no idea what it might be. Like the medical consultant, there was something about Emma's come-through that pointed three degrees off true north, but nothing specific.

That was the problem as Emma's stay dragged into the fifteenth day— nothing specific. The ulcerations continued their march, worsening and ebbing through time and place, affecting different parts of Emma's body without distinguishable pattern. Emma herself had now become a low-grade celebrity, visited by all medical students and most of the department heads. She had been subjected to nearly every test imaginable, including MRIs, plasma electrophoresis, and ultrascans. Her low-grade fever continued unabated.

On the morning of the sixteenth day, just after Emma had been rolled off to radiology, Doris Evenston arrived on her rounds to make up Emma's bed. Doris, a recently hired employee, took her bed-making very seriously. Unlike some housekeeping personnel, Doris made sure the sheets were well secured, tucking them deeply in between the box spring and mattress. Reaching under the mattress to nearly her elbows while tucking in the sheets, Doris let out a surprised "Ouch!" She felt herself unexpectedly pricked in her middle finger. The puncture was deep enough that there was blood staining the sheets when she pulled her arm out from between mattress and boxspring. Housekeeping personnel in hospitals are not known for going out of their way to satisfy their curiosity. But Doris, after washing off her finger, resolutely returned to the bed and started pulling the mattress off the bedspring to discover what in the world down there had punctured her finger. She was starting to pull the mattress off its support when Emma, pushed by an aide, arrived back at the door of the room in her wheel chair.

"WHAT IN THE WORLD ARE YOU DOING?!"

Doris explained that she had been jabbed in the finger by something way down deep under the mattress and was determined to find out what it might have been.

Emma huffed, "Well, you can look for that later. Right now I'm exhausted from being x-rayed. Come back another time."

"I still need to change the sheets," Donna said hesitantly.

"But not NOW," Emma demanded.

That did it. Donna had her *duty!* When Emma demanded she come back later, Donna's back stiffened. No siree, no patient was going to order a hospital *employee* around. Donna insisted on making Emma's bed *now.* While doing so, for good measure she heaved up on the mattress, peering back beneath it as far as she could. Between mattress and box spring she spied a small rectangular tin. She reached in and pulled it out. It was a tin of Rosignol lighter fluid. (In those days, smoking was common, and lighter fluid was common in many homes.) Lighter fluid? Donna stood looking at it, baffled. It just didn't compute. Neither fires nor smoking was allowed in the room. Someone had stuck that can of lighter fluid way back under that mattress. It was then that Donna noticed the absolutely horrified look on Emma Alseron's face. Donna had no idea what this was all about, but she knew darn well from that look on the face that Emma had something to do with it.

"What's this?" she asked, still in some shock.

"I don't know," Emma stammered.

That did it for Donna. She knew that anyone's dead brother would recognize the familiar yellow and blue can of Rosignol lighter fluid. She

16

was emboldened to search further beneath the mattress for the object that had stabbed her finger and with eagle eye spied a glass syringe and needle.

Later the internist said to me, "Damn, I thought those sores smelled kinda funny sometimes."

I apologized, "Gees, Ted, I thought the lady might be holding back, but honestly, I had no idea she was so far out that she'd inject herself with lighter fluid."

Everyone realized in retrospect that all of Emma's sores, all over her body, did have one distinguishing characteristic. They were all within easy reach of both hands. That could have been a tip off.

Emma did indeed appear to be a good candidate for psychiatric intervention, but I was rotating off the unit. That thankless job would be left to my replacement to handle on an outpatient basis, providing, of course, that Emma would even make her appointments. Successful hypochondriacs don't much cotton to change. More likely she'd move to new digs and run the *same game, new chapter* with a different clinic in a different city, stumping new docs. Obviously she wasn't getting enough attention from her cats.

4. IF NANCY DIVORCES ME, I WILL KILL YOU BOTH!

Nancy came to see me when she was in her mid-thirties, a tall, nicely groomed brunette. Truth be told, a very pretty lady. She came to me in the midst of chronic marital difficulties, claiming that Jake was verbally and physically abusive. She came alone, insisting that Jake had assured her there "was no way in hell" that he was going to see another counselor with her. Considering that she had squeezed through fifteen unhappy years married to Jake, she wore her thirty years with minimal physical meltdown well and was generally able to keep her psychological scars from making an ugly appearance.

I learned that around town, outside the marriage, old Jake was a hearty, gregarious sort of fellow. He was well-liked at Rotary and palled around with guys in town who liked to fish and hunt.

As with many abusive husbands, he was seen by their mutual friends as a basically nice guy and often "the life of the party." This common perception leads those abused to feel very much alone, because when a victimized spouse, girlfriend, or boyfriend does work up the courage to tell someone about their relationship hell, the response is shock bordering on disbelief. In this case, it would be, "You've got to be kidding.... Not Jake!" And even if the sad situation is believed, others may understandably wonder, "What in the world did Nancy do to get a nice guy like Jake to act like that!?"

Nancy told a story of a marriage filled with more than verbal abuse. She claimed Jake had beat her up on a number of occasions, leaving enough black and blue marks that she was ashamed to go to work. The night before seeing me for the first time, Jake had screamed at her, insisting that all the problems in the marriage were "by God, your issues, Nancy!" That night, hunkering terrified on the floor and begging him not to hurt her, she made the decision to see yet another therapist. Of course I did not know it then but I found out later that she felt seeing me would probably be fruitless.

Before coming to Colorado, the couple endured an unhappy marriage in Chicago, where Jake had bounced from job to job while their relationship deteriorated over the five years they lived there. Both wished for a new start in a new environment and because Nancy's brother lived in town and had she insisted on moving where she might find support. And as a matter of fact, she did get support, for I was acquainted professionally with her brother, who for months had urged his sister to see me.

As most abused spouses, Nancy had lived for years in the lonely world between a rock and a hard spot. Understandably, like most, she had prayed that her situation would improve and she could live like all the others that surrounded her—relationships that she envied and wanted for herself. But, as almost always, as the years passed the rock only grew harder and the hard spot, rockier.

Many, as did Nancy, after the third or fourth escalating beating, seek help. Sometimes the cops are called. But cops don't like being called for marital problems. Sometimes that's the situation that gets cops killed. And to law enforcement's absolute consternation, after calming down the situation, they find that the abused person often refuses to press charges. Of course, the angry and disappointed cops may only be vaguely aware of something the spouse, boyfriend, or girlfriend knows very well indeed: "After I press charges, and after he gets out of jail a few days later, he'll come back and kill me!"

Occasionally it may be helpful to take out a restraining order, but bad boys and girls often don't have a passion for sticking to the law. In fact, many of the folks are knocked off by an angry spouse not sticking to the terms of their restraining order. Serving some spouses with a restraint order is akin to controlling the beehive by poking at it with a stick.

As I noted, after a final harrowing nighttime scare, Nancy first came in to see me. I phoned Jake. I was pretty good at getting nasty, blaming, and reluctant spouses to come in because I often approached them with a conspiratorial little white lie rather than the truth. The truth would be something along the lines: "I've seen your spouse and you've been acting like a jerk. Come on in; we'll get to work and see if you can't trip off toward a more pleasant life with other people." But truth tends not to work.

I phoned Jake and started right out using the white lies that often worked so successfully with nasty partners. This basic approach, of course, has to be explained and cleared with the client first. Nancy thought the approach was a fine idea and that it might work like magic with Jake.

"Jake, I've seen Nancy a couple of times. I understand your concerns. Boy, this lady can be a real handful, can't she!? I really need your take on the situation in order to help her. I just can't do it by myself. So will you help me out with her?"

Almost always, after first agreeing to come in just to help me get their spouse's head together, both form a trusting relationship with me and I can usually help happier times begin to unroll.

But Jake was a tough cookie: Throughout that first conversation, Jake, with

19

obvious effort, maintained a veneer of civility about as thick as a thin coat of shellac.

"Look, doc, I don't appreciate this call. I told Nancy that she'd have to figure out her shit for herself. I went with her to see another therapist in Chicago, and I'm not going to put myself through your psycho-babble again."

An earlier therapist? That was new information! "You went with her to see a therapist in Chicago?"

"Damn straight! And it didn't help a bit. If anything, it made things a lot worse."

"Well, Jake, not all therapists operate similarly. I really do need your help with this. Look, if you don't like the way things are going, or if you feel seeing me isn't helpful, you can always quit. Seeing me is pretty fail-safe."

Silly me! I was talking, of course, about the situation being fail-safe for Jake and Nancy. I had no idea what would be roaring full tilt down the pike at me!

Protesting and with great reluctance, Jake agreed to come in with Nancy on the following day.

During that session, much to my surprise, their viewpoints were congruent. They agreed on almost everything! Nancy maintained that Jake was downright mean, arrogant, demanding, and at times frightening. He agreed fully. She said he didn't really want to change, and he agreed. She said she had tried really, really hard to make things work…and he agreed!

In short, Jake agreed that he was simply an arrogant, demanding, son-of-a-bitch, but that Nancy had made the choice to live with him, and now she needed to shut up and make the best of the situation. During the session, it came out that Nancy had tried calling the police in Chicago and it had ended in disaster. Jake was quick to note, "I like to have killed her for that."

After an hour of zero progress, Jake made sure I knew that my input was about as helpful as grease on pig-catching day. I told Nancy that I'd see her the following week.

All week, I mulled over her untenable situation. It seemed obvious to me that she was in a dangerous situation that could worsen over time. If Jake had been a run-of-the-mill bipolar person, or simply acting out of desperation, that would have been different. There is real hope in hopelessness! But Jake's problem was more of a life stance. He insisted, and I agreed, that his primary diagnosis was JPM. And people who are Just Plain Mean don't need a psychiatrist. The college of hard knocks or jail tends to be more therapeutic.

I forgot to ask them about the therapist they had seen in Chicago.

Now I'm a great believer in working things out within a marriage. But in the cases of verifiable and serious abuse carried out by character-disturbed spouses, the best answer is sometimes to advise a gal or guy to get the heck out of Dodge. I advised Nancy when I next saw her to file for divorce and plan to live a less dangerous life.

"Nancy, I have told you that I think most couples, most of the time, can learn to live happily together. But I don't think that applies to your situation. How seriously have you really considered divorce?"

Nancy started crying and said that her psychiatrist in Chicago, the one that Jake evidently hated, had given the same advice. She surprised me by saying, "I just didn't want you to know about it, because I knew you would want to go into it. And I didn't want you to know what he said." Tears continued to flow.

"Well, I don't want to necessarily pry into what he said, but if he said you should get a divorce, why wouldn't I want to know about that?"

Following that simple question, Nancy's sobbing escalated to a torrent of wet sorrow. Her expression sagged and she buried her face in her hands, leaking tears between her fingers before I could get the Kleenex. I knew the idea of getting a divorce can be very upsetting, even to wives who have suffered serious abuse, but gosh, her sobs were heart rending—more than most women in this situation.

"Why are you crying so hard?"

"You're telling me to get a divorce…. That's what Dr. Cole in Chicago said. He said, 'Nancy, the *only way* out of this situation for you is to get a divorce.'"

"Bright guy. Why didn't you?"

"I'm coming to that…. Jake phoned Dr. Cole and told him that if he didn't change his recommendation, he'd kill him. The next time I saw Dr. Cole, he did change his recommendation and told me I'd have to stay with Jake if we both wanted to live. So that's what I've done."

Gees! Scarrreey! I have to admit, I hesitated, but then, hoping to quench the Niagara of unhappiness, I said, "Nancy, I'll stick to my guns on this and I'll talk to Jake." This brave front was mostly, I'm sure, successful at hiding the chill I felt underneath. "You just tell the cops about this situation, head off to a safe house, get a *very* good lawyer, and *don't back down*."

Worriedly, she said, "What about you?"

"You let me worry about that!" These brave words ignored the fact that all through my gut thousands of butterfly hatchlings were struggling out of their cocoons.

That evening, my wife Hermie told me that I looked distracted. But then again, visions of being shot or run down can do that. I responded, "Well, I've had an interesting day." And I thought that if I lived through it, I'd tell her about it someday. No sense scaring the living daylights out of her, too. The butterflies did not settle down, and while they fluttered away after I went to bed, I lay there awake imagining the variety of ways that I could make an excellent murder victim.

And then about midnight, a plan began to form in my mind.

I had hardly arrived in at the office the next morning when my secretary buzzed me on the intercom and said, "Jake Andersen is on the phone and he sounds super mad. He wants an appointment with you. And, Foster, he even cursed at *me*!" I told Elizabeth to make the appointment for the first thing in the afternoon.

And then I told her about my plan. She was a little doubtful and perhaps a little scared, but she said she could carry it out.

That afternoon, at 1:00, right on schedule, Jake banged into the office, slamming the door and telling Elizabeth that he wanted to see the damn psychiatrist *now*. Elizabeth assured him that I was waiting.

With invectives and superlatives laced with obscenities, Jake assured me that unless I talked Nancy out of the divorce, I would not have long to live. I was pretty quiet and did not have much to say, which led Jake to roll on and add threateningly that he would make my death look like an accident.

I listened respectfully to Jake. I empathized with him about how hard life might be for him at first after Nancy left. I tried to help him understand that there were other women out there that he could marry. (Of course, that was an outright lie because, with Jake's history, any woman agreeing to marry him would not have a working circuit upstairs. Word tends to get around!)

After about twenty minutes, and finding and that nothing I said could extinguish Jake's fulminating rage and threats, I decided to put my plan into action:

I reached over and touched the intercom. "Elizabeth, are you there?"

"Right here."

"Have you been listening?"

"Yeah, I have it all on tape, Foster."

I turned again to Jake. "You see, Jake, you have a problem. If you knock me off now, you won't be able to claim irresistible impulse. You won't be able to claim temporary insanity. And if I die through some accident, the cops are going to crawl all over you. This is your problem. You'll without doubt fry for first-degree murder. Your whole problem will be that you can't deny that you planned it all out, made threats, and carried it out. Jurors aren't going to treat you nice after listening to this tape, Jake. There's no way you can beat the rap."

At first I thought that maybe Jake hadn't heard me, 'cause he just sat there very, very quiet. Too quiet. It was unsettling. Perhaps he was going to pounce right then.

Then, to my utter shock, he said, "You got me, doc. You're smarter than I thought."

Really! I was concerned that this might be some kind of trick. That perhaps Jake would jump up and try to threaten Elizabeth into giving him the tape, or threaten her directly.

Buried like a maggot, afraid of the light, hopelessness almost always lies squiggling beneath rage. So, right or wrong, I took Jake's continued silence as an opportunity for me to describe a future possible trip down hopeful lane. "Jake, a lot of people in this town seem to like you. You've done a lot of good at Rotary. You have your whole life ahead of you, and although I don't know you all that well, I can see that you could have a lot brighter future than ending up this young in some crematorium. I've helped a lot of guys and gals go through their divorces and they're often happier. That could be true of you."

Jake didn't say another word. He just sat there very quietly. It seemed like a very long time. But I'll bet it wasn't more than twenty very tense seconds. Then he just got up and walked out. And that's the last I ever saw or heard of Jake.

Nancy immediately packed it in and got out of town. Bright girl. I kept in touch with her brother, and over the following years Nancy became a happy camper living in a city to the west. She remarried.

Oh, I did see Jake one more time. He passed me once in his pickup truck, with his hunting rifles happily displayed across the rack in the back window. He looked over, directly at me, and I thought he might be giving the message, "No need to relax yet, doc. I'm waiting."

But years ago, when dealing with others like Jake, I learned that most psychopaths, way down deep, are cowards. They bluster and threaten to harm others, but if you get your ducks in a row and stand up to them, they generally back down.

5. GERMS HOPPED OFF THE SCISSORS
AND INFECTED THE WHOLE HOUSE

Into the King County Psychiatric Emergency Service wandered the
walking wounded of Washington State's Emerald City. They are unhinged
people from Seattle's streets, angry people crawling out from beneath the
overpasses and bridges, and of course, those newly released from either
prison or the state hospital. Some resentful and others just sad, they all
tended to blame twists of uncaring fate. Most of the sad, resentful, angry,
and wounded, however, were living out the results of a lifetime of poor
choices. Most usually wandered into the King County Hospital's
emergency entrance in the middle of the night: the depressed, the
homeless, the unhappy, the paranoid, and the dangerous. And most from
Seattle's lower socio-economic belly.

Night seems to collect those with severe chronic problems, and the bright
fluorescent county emergency entrances are the light that attracts, like
moths, those who circle and flutter in. Betty had always been drawn the
emergency room at night. I don't think she had ever had a daytime visit.

Though out history, dark humor has helped humanity bear up through
harrowing and difficult situations, whether in the MASH operating room of
a field hospital or in WWI trenches. It is understandable that folks can be
judgmental of such dark humor. It is hard for those who have not lived
through harrowing experiences to comprehend a coping mechanism they,
themselves, have never needed to use.

Thus, bantering between physicians and nurses about those who might be
expected to grace the ER on full-moon nights filled slow minutes of early
evenings. Ribbing would take place, nurse to physician: "Hey, Foster wait
'til you meet Betty. She'll show you what life in the great Never-Never
Land is all about." A ripple of anticipation would flow through the nursing
staff as they gleefully looked forward to the arrival of very difficult clients.
These patients would likely provide the nursing staff with an interesting
all-night peep show as Dr. New Meat, aroused from a sound sleep, would
attempt to cope with some Pike Street challenge. Every night was different,
and the influx, depending on the moon phase, truly gave new meaning to
the word "lunacy."

A pale, shuffling Betty Brown made her monthly visits to the emergency
room, arriving with a disjointed stew of crazy, sucky and demanding
emotions. She had the reputation of keeping most initiates up all night. She
always refused admission, but also refused to leave. And like many

controlling psychiatric patients, she could become noisy—*real noisy*—when she didn't get her way.

Diagnostically, Betty was diagnosed "Borderline." This diagnosis is often reserved for folks forever living in the twilight of sanity. Borderline people, often women, aren't crazy in the usual sense. They are crazy-canny-controlling. They control by suicide threats and whining demands. The metaphor is a person who hugs you closer while holding a stiletto to your navel. Folks with this diagnosis might wake up helping professionals in the middle of the night to complain on the phone that they can't sleep. After yanking a friend or professional through a very unpleasant conversation, a Borderline person might often refuse to hang up. In the bad old Ma Bell days a land phone line was forever open until the *calling* party broke it. Individuals had been known to hang on the phone for hours.

Before telling of my introduction to Betty, I must briefly describe two books that influenced me greatly prior to that memorable meeting.

About the time I rotated into King County Hospital, I read a little green tome called *Principles of Psychotherapy* by Jay Haley. Haley was a pretty interesting guy. He had provocative ideas for relating to crazy people. Haley was basically a communication theorist and felt that psychotic or crazy behavior often simply served as a control mechanism for interpersonal relationships. He wrote that everyone, way down deep, wants to relate to others and to have some control of those relationships. Many children grow up in a home where healthy and usual methods of interaction don't work.

Healthy people are up front about the give and take of relationships. But when children grow up in disturbed homes, communication is often muddled. Who calls the shots and who is in control of a relationship become both important and fuzzy. Haley felt that some psychotics choose craziness as a way of staying in control of a relationship. The controlling person peeps out of Neverland, and the other, whether a frustrated spouse or professional responding from Realsville, attempts to engage in a reality-based conversation and then loses all control of the situation. In refusing to leave the world of irrationality, the disturbed person inevitably controls. Most rationals are not at all adroit at relating to irrationals. On the other hand, many irrationals have had considerable practice driving the sane absolutely crazy.

But Haley insisted that there might be a way to pry open the door into Neverland and lead folks to reality, to relate and even beneficially take control of a psychotic conversation, bringing an individual back to sanity. He maintained that each inner crazy world is an individualistic theme park with only room for one on any ride. The world of a psychotic, he maintained, is as personal to that individual as the Sistine Chapel was to Michelangelo. So, two folks cannot inhabit the same crazy landscape at the same time.

At about that time, too, I read Robert Lindner's little book, *The Fifty Minute Hour.* Lindner was a New York author and psychiatrist. And evidently a good therapist—his little book was a bestseller. It made for pretty interesting reading. One chapter was filled with his experience inadvertently driving a crazy patient sane by entering his patient's world and talking crazy. It reminded me of Jay Haley's communication theories.

Lindner wrote of a paranoid patient who insisted he was captain of a spaceship. Lindner somehow honestly slid from curious to excited and became an active participant, himself drawing star charts of his own galactic jaunts. To his patient's increasing consternation, it appeared that Lindner had a faster ship and had visited even further galactic suburbs. Within a few weeks, the patient was pleading, "Dr. Lindner, all this isn't *real.* I just made it all up, honest." I guess it can be pretty unnerving when your psychiatrist starts acting sicker than you. Maybe it depends on how much he's charging. New York psychiatrists were pricey, even then.

So all this Haley and Lindner writing was bumping around in the recesses of my cerebrum when Betty Brown, with the onset of a full moon, wandered into the King County ER.

Janice, the head nurse down in the ER, awoke me from my sound sleep in the on-call room. I was almost certain there was a gleeful undertone to her professional request. "Dr. Cline, we have a walk-in requesting to see the psychiatrist on call."

I picked up that staff in the ER were ready for a fun-filled vicarious evening of "Watch Betty drive the new doc crazy." A bit of bravado was called for and I gamely responded: "Glad you woke me up. Thanks. I was having a nightmare."

To my surprise, a little of her professionalism slipped, and with evident false concern, she hung up saying, "After the next two hours, you'll like your nightmare better. Plan on being up all night, Foster."

Hustling through the ER area, I endured the side-glances of the three on-duties. Janice said mockingly, "Have fun, Foster."

I entered the exam room.

"What's the problem, Miss Brown?"

Betty was hunched over the exam table. While she didn't flow all over it

27

like a lot of the inner city night belles, she was well built, and if not for her complete lack of eye contact and animation could have been a heavy but pretty young lady. Her skin was a little gray. Her eyes were vacant and as flat as her voice. Often speaking softly and staring down, she shoved out her words and they simply haltingly dripped onto the floor. And she had a quiet rasping pant, almost as if she had a difficult experience hauling herself over the wall and out of Neverland to come to the hospital.

Words were strung out, inflectionless, individually dumped onto the floor like disconnected Legos spilled from a child's hand. Not rolling out, but with a steady, hard, unending, disconnected stream that had a suffocating quality.

To hear this young woman dropping out this inflectionless string of words was enough to make any young physician feel a little unsettled as he or she peeped across the bridge into his patient's flat, colorless, stale, and unhappy world. Her nearly pretty appearance, coupled with her crazy story that I'm about to relate, was totally incongruous.

The story, as it turned out, was well known to the entire emergency room staff. Betty Brown had a problem with germs. They infested her entire home.

The story of her problems with germs crawled out from her mouth and splattered onto the ER floor in a monotone that had hints of buried anger. I could only sit and listen, for there was no pause as her words, which, like the germs she spoke of, seemed to contaminate the exam room. On a flat implacable roll, she didn't even leave room for the professional "hummm" that I had learned so well, and with practice, to utter thoughtfully in my first year of training.

I can only give the reader a feeling of her flat monotone if I write her words without punctuation. Imagine for yourself, as you read this, how you might feel listening to this young woman as she stared at floor, bent over, talking softly without pause.

"There are germs everywhere in my home because my mother washed my panties in the washing machine and after they were washed my mother took her sewing needle and sewed up this little hole in the crotch of my panties and I begged mother to be careful with that needle and thread but my mother did not listen to me and she cut the thread with her sewing scissors although I warned her not to use those scissors and I said 'mother do not use those sewing scissors to cut other thread just throw them away' but my mother did not listen to me and used those same sewing scissors to cut thread that she used to repair doilies and napkins and other things and she cut cloth with those sewing scissors and I said 'mother you cannot use those scissors because they cut the thread that had been used to sew up my panties after they had been washed' and I said 'mother look what you are doing' but my mother paid no attention to me and soon the germs from the thread used to mend the doilies spread over the whole living room and I said 'mother what have you done' but she just tells me not to worry about the germs but I know they are there because she washes those doilies in the washing machine with other things she washes spreading the germs to sheets and covers and I warned her but still my mother will not listen to me...."

There seemed no way to staunch the onslaught of words. The words just kept dripping out in an unending flat monologue.

It didn't take therapeutic wizardry to figure out a couple things.

There were certainly psychodynamic underpinnings to this unhappy flow, probably conscious or unconscious concerns about sexuality, as the hole in Betty's panties was the pebble of concern around which her pearl of craziness was constructed. Certainly my Freudian predecessors in training and many other professionals in the outpatient clinics had followed that track down a rabbit hole.

And of course, under her flat effect, which lacked the animation of damp Plaster of Paris, there was likely hatred of her mother. The growth and spread of the ubiquitous little germs was totally her mom's fault. Her mom wouldn't listen to her. Her mom didn't take her seriously.

The kind of flatness Betty displayed on the surface often covers deep and seething hidden feelings. Such feelings are too terrifying to face. I didn't have to be Dr. Insightful to know that the Neverland where she lived was likely a swamp of oozing rage, hate, and sexual issues.

Another thing, too, was obvious: Her story was finely honed. It was a sort of obvious, *in-your-face* type of craziness. Betty made sure she had clarified that her panties had been washed before being sewed up. And the germs happily migrated through the entire house after first scampering onto the scissors from the snipped sewing thread. After vacationing a bit on the scissor blades they evidently jumped everywhere.

I thought of the many young resident physicians who had sat where I was sitting. And all to no avail. Here in the middle of the night was evidence that their interpretations and efforts to talk-sanity-to-Betty had been totally ineffective. Those approaches must have been trod by her mother and a dozen others: "Betty, your panties were washed. Germs probably wouldn't live on a piece of thread and if they did, they wouldn't hang out on those scissors." On and on. I knew that the interpretation and the let's-reason-this-out tack had been followed previously in the clinic and Betty had undoubtedly, as the night wore on, grown louder, more certain of her infection, and ever more controlling. She would deny problems with her mom and would have kept control of the situation by refusing to be helped.

As Betty droned on without inflection or pause, I thought of Jay Haley's little green book. I thought of Lindner writing of driving crazy clients sane by talking crazy. So I took a deep breath and interrupted her flat flow of words. I said with a certainty I didn't feel,

"I know what your problem is, Betty."

Shockingly, she paused. "You do?" Her voice had a new quality, perhaps only four clicks short of surprise.

For those of you interested, I've found that it is not always effective to speak sweetly and with political correctness to angry, distant, and rejecting folks.

It was undoubtedly futile to slog along the same path others had certainly previously trod. I was pretty darn certain that at least no one had taken *this* path. I almost held my breath. "Yeah, Betty, I do know your problem…. I think you have a *very dirty crotch.*"

In response, Betty's flat speech suddenly came to a halt. With some inflection, even boarding on animation she asked, "How can you say that!?"

"Well, the panties were washed. And they were still evidently filthy."

"My panties weren't filthy!" Was there some kind of spark in those dead, flat eyes?

"Well, they were Betty. And think about how the germs migrated from the thread and clung to those scissors. There must have been millions."

Surprisingly, a flush flowed across the previously chalk gray face. Real anger was trying to claw its way into her voice. "Germs can't live on scissors!"

"Well, way down there, Betty, in the *crotch* of the scissors, there was probably a little rust. That's where the germs hung out."

"Germs don't live on rust."

"How do you know? Have you ever looked at rust though a microscope?"

Resentfully: "No."

"Well, there you go. Are you saying I don't know what I'm talking about?"

"Maybe."

"Well then, why the heck are you seeing me! Why are we talking? What's going on here? You trot in and tell me what the problem is, and I agree. I'm just telling you how it all happens. Don't blame me if you have a dirty crotch!"

Betty was a different gal. Her eyes flashed. Her voice was strong, and she sat straight. She had been hunched like some gargoyle on top of Westminster. Not anymore!

"There is no way I have a dirty crotch! I don't like it when you say that."

"Well, what would you like me to say?"

"You're the psychiatrist. You tell me."

"Well, you agree that you came in here to tell me about germs from your crotch. So where do you want to start?

"Look, I have other problems than germs!"

"Really! What might those be?"

With that simple question, to my surprise, Betty trounced right out of Neverland and into the light. She talked about her little room in her mom's home and how she hated living there. She had to get out. She wanted help getting a job. She was bored with life. Maybe that even played a role in pestering other people about germs.

Forty-five minutes later when we opened the door and stepped out of the exam room, Betty trounced out walking straight and downright animated. Shocking me with a smile and quick high five, she then thanked both me and the nurses for putting up with her on other occasions and said she'd be coming back tomorrow for a follow-up. She liked seeing me! The staff was far beyond flabbergasted.

"Foster, what in the world did you say to her?"

"Janice," I pontificated, yet with proper *aw shucks* humility, "some problems lie very, very deep. Way, way, down in depths of the psyche. You wouldn't want to go there in one of your nightmares. "

From there on out I could do no wrong with those nurses in the ER. And I thank Haley and Lindner, who were such a help.

6. CLIMBING GREEN POLES

The tall thin telephone lineman didn't decide to pop in for therapy on his own. The supervisor down at the phone company had *strongly* suggested he get some help for his nerves. He worked outdoors. He looked it. Carl was angular, thin, and appeared a little rough and weather-beaten around the edges. His resting expression was kind of hang-dog. He traveled through life with the common combination of free-floating anger commingled with a bit of depression. So with his supervisor hinting that his job was on the line, he had little choice but to arrive at someone's waiting room. Living in Evergreen, it was natural that he would seek help at Evergreen Consultants. A cloud of unhappiness curled around him most of the month or so that I saw him in the office. It was certainly evident the December day we met.

He said his name was Carl and he worked for Ma Bell. In those days there were no cell phones and everyone depended on reliable phone lines. Carl spent time high off the ground—often on wet, cold poles in the winter following a snowstorm, providing the rest of us with the phone service we had come to expect even when icy lines grew heavy and dropped to the ground. Carl was dissatisfied with most of life: job, wife, and kids. But what really, really, upset him, and the reason his supervisor insisted he get help, were his malevolent and resentful complaints about the necessary requirements of his job.

Although mainly across-the-board dissatisfied, he most resolutely focused his ire on the new telephone poles the company had erected up and down the mountain roads of Jefferson County. To protect them from the weather, the new greenish poles were impregnated with chemicals, rather than the old previously used globby black tarry creosote. Carl was irate in his condemnation of the green poles: "Damn new poles are slick. My boot cleats can't grab a tight hold on that green shit. Someone's going to fall climbing those damn things. The company is going to have the shit sued out of them. And they should."

He accused the company, probably incorrectly, of not giving a rip if his cold dead body was found at the base of one of those green giants. With agitation he said, "And I've warned 'em. Warned 'em more than once. Buyin' them poles was one of the poorest damn decisions they ever made." Then he would launch into a fusillade of other complaints regarding management decisions. When his focus wandered from management inadequacies, as it often did, he would complain about his wife and the "rat pack" of kids at home. He said his wife, in bed, showed him the warmth of a trout in a winter stream. Their sexual relationship was filled with almost as much conflict as their differences about handling the rat pack. Carl, who lived a life of perennial disappointment on the job, felt doubly cheated when he could not pop home to a castle with a fire in the hearth, a sweet wife, and thoughtful children.

More than once, as I recall, I emphasized that *I was a shrink*. Therefore I worked on what was *inside* of folks. I couldn't do much about the management decisions that old Ma Bell made about buying green telephone poles. True, Carl needed to make some decisions about whether or not he was distressed enough to change jobs. I could help him sort out those options. However, there were the *important* things around character and family that could usefully be focused upon. As would any psychiatrist, I made sure we discussed the unhappy truth that whether on top of a pole, tightening a wire, or working out an electrical outage, the sad truth was that Carl would always have Carl for company! His disgruntled personality would check with him into any job. So he ought to think about working on that. And for that he had come to the right place!

With only minor therapeutic prodding, Carl agreed with the wisdom of my consultations, and, in the following weeks, we began the more essential journey of tripping through his personality development, parenting tools and skills, and marital relationship issues.

His angry feelings had first been expressed in his unhappy childhood. He recalled how his dad had frightened the hell out of him by locking him in the coal cellar as a kid. That grew out of a fight about going to a St. Patrick's Day parade! All the puzzle pieces of his anger over green poles appeared to fit nicely. His Irish dad's favorite color was green, and he made a big deal out of wearing green and going to the parade every St. Patrick's Day.

We moved on efficiently to good old Love and Logic® parenting skills and tools that would be useful to Carl and his wife, Laura, as they learned to discipline the rat pack effectively. I counseled both parents on several occasions. Thing were generally humming along quite nicely and I was as pleased as a herring in white sauce about his improved family life with wife and kids. Carl, of course, never really got over his fear of climbing "those damn green poles," However, he liked the Ma Bell retirement and health bennies enough that he decided not to bag his lineman job. So, Carl graduated from therapy.

Not that he was a pool of happiness. He still spent too much time grumbling, but he was functioning a heck of a lot better and was even low-grade pleased with himself much of the time. He and Laura's relationship improved and the kids straightened out. This was no miracle cure, that's for sure, and Carl's old job irritation would often leak around the corners of his day-to-day life. But after all, character issues around anger don't disappear like morning mists on the North Platte.

Several years after last seeing Carl, I was pleasantly surprised to meet him as we were both picking out vegetables in the Evergreen Safeway store.

"Oh, hi, doc!"

"Hey, Carl, how's it going?"

We exchanged pleasantries for a bit, during which Carl mentioned that he had seen Dr. Campbell, and "*he* really helped me." That "he" was emphasized far too meaningfully, I thought.

I asked, "Did you see him for a very long time?"

"No, just once."

I told him that I was happy to hear that Dr. Campbell had been such a help. And I did have to admit that Carl himself did seem, if not bubbling, at least relaxed and happy. Truthfully, being mercilessly honest with myself, he appeared more relaxed than during the six weeks or so that I had been seeing him.

Of course I was truly happy Dr. Campbell had helped him. But other feelings were peeking around the edges of my midbrain. Dr. Campbell was "just" an old family practitioner. He wasn't even trained in counseling. How could he have been *that* much help that fast? It was downright unsettling. I stood contemplating the asparagus as long as I could without looking appearing completely zoned out while collecting my thoughts and sorting through my feelings.

It would be a little embarrassing to ask.

But if I didn't ask, I'd always wonder. So I screwed up my courage and looked around for Carl. By this time, he had happily migrated to the potatoes.

"Hey, Carl, I'm just wondering. If you don't mind, tell me what Dr. Campbell did that helped you so much?"

Carl was happy to enlighten me. His answer stunned me. Why, oh why, hadn't I thought of that?

"Doc, you remember those damn green poles? That was what *really* bothered me. Well, Dr. Campbell wrote me a prescription so I wouldn't have to climb those things."

7. CONTAMINATION

If you should ever find yourself looking for a mental health professional, let me give you a heads up. You may not realize that your best chance for success may depend on your mental health professional being *at least* as healthy as you are! I'm not kidding. All too often the professionals just don't have their heads together themselves. You don't believe me?! Check it out for yourself. Just wander into the nearest high school classroom and ask members of the graduating class, "Who of you want to become therapists or counselors?" If you think for one moment that the class Valedictorian is going to raise her or his hand, you're in for a surprise. The really healthy kids want to go into physics, electrical engineering, nursing, or teaching—usually they long for anything other than becoming a mental health professional.

When you ask the question, do check out the kids who may be waving their arms in the air. The hands and arms of the dysfunctional kids from broken, possibly abusive homes will wave in the air like a field of daisies in a spring breeze. Those waving hands are really saying, "Me, me! I want to be a counselor because my dad beat the living daylights out of me and I'm screwed up and very angry because of it." Many of these youth identify with victims, advocate for victims, and often encourage feelings of victimization wherever they go. Without realizing it, many workers in the departments of social services have a *need* to find abuse, and I saw literally dozens of families destroyed because of false accusations of abuse and professional response that has to be labeled harassment.

During the eighties there were gaggles of women's groups, often led by one or another female therapist, who, abused by her dad and four times divorced, made a living helping other women achieve better relationships by "getting in touch" with their loving and sensitive side. One very well-known social worker sort of clarified the situation with her comment, "Of course I'm an expert on marital relationships, I've been married six times!" Looking for parenting advice from someone? You could do yourself a favor by meeting their kids. If you, yourself, wouldn't want to take those little hellions off the shelf, you might consider finding another professional. Think you might be in trouble in the old marital relationship? It would be both delightful and wise to choose a therapist who has married fewer than four times, who has been married for longer than two years, and who had had a loving relationship with his or her spouse. I know, I know, this sounds sort of like common sense. However, folks tend to put more energy into researching a new refrigerator than they do into choosing their

35

mental health professionals.

Now that we've been considering the idea of checking out the mental health professionals, we come to my own problem!

It has to do with the second thing you might hope for. You might hope your therapist is honest about how his or her personal beliefs and morals could influence the way you are treated.

When I first went into training, most mental health professionals declared with certainty that their beliefs would not and should not affect their treatment. It has been the opposite in medically related fields. Obstetricians and pharmacists have been very upfront when they insist that patients they serve adhere to the provider's value system. For instance, there has been national attention given to stories of regretful young women who admit to making a mistake and the obstetrician or pharmacist refuses to provide a prescription for a "morning after" pill—purely on the basis of their own beliefs. In essence they say, "Live with the child you don't want. Live with him or her for the next 18 years." Or, "Carry the child around for nine months; go through the pain and expense of morning sickness, low back pain, and birth trauma, and then put yourself through the agony of giving your baby away. You see, my dear, that little sperm swimming upstream in you might meet an egg, and the egg might be fertilized, and it might then cling onto your uterus, and then it might grow, and I don't believe in killing people!" Hey, I understand. It's not the professional's daughter! However, after meeting a number of such professionals, I have a hunch that most would have no problem with giving their own daughter a prescription if she were in the same situation and it was their own unwanted grandchild they might be saddled with.

I started out not being that aware of one of my beliefs and how it could affect my therapy. But Sally straightened me out, and I learned from her. Let me lay the foundation now:

We mental health professionals are encouraged tend the slippery slopes of mental health, burying our personal beliefs in order to hone in on the facts, no more influenced by our own pasts than a river rock is influenced by the flow of the water around it. We're only supposed to provide what the patient wants and needs, not what our own morals, beliefs, personal pasts, or personal tastes dictate. This was harped on in endlessly in our training: *"Don't let your personal beliefs contaminate how you respond to people."* Our university psychiatric professors nearly salivated with joy when they could use that *"contaminate"* term. *"Contaminate!"* The very word conjures up sterile operating rooms. That's where *real* medicine takes place! Psychiatrists, you see, are the physicians that live on the wrong side of the track…they're not *real* physicians. So that medical term, *contaminate,* helped our professors assure themselves, and everyone around, that they were, by God, real doctors too! Our old profs spit out "contaminate" with such frequency and derision that one might think they were worried about every young therapist coughing uncovered in their treatment rooms! *"Don't contaminate your therapy."*

I was pretty darn sure that I would never *contaminate* my therapy. Of course, that turned out not to be true. And as I said, I needed to learn that. It happened like this:

Less than a year after I'd begun my practice, Sally and Harold arrived for their first appointment. Although they excelled at marital fighting, they were nevertheless growing weary of unending spats. Even when folks are experts at something, it can get old.

They had every right to be unhappy with each other. Sally grew up the only child of an angry, verbally abusive father and Harold the only son of a demanding and controlling mother. By the time both were teens, they had become unconscious experts at forming relationships with people they could easily grow to hate. I'm certain that from the time of their first meeting, he was demanding and she was critical. Obviously, such a match made in heaven led them to fall madly in love, and as both wanted out of their parents' house, they were soon married. He unconsciously wanted and got a girl just like the girl that married dear old dad.

When both individuals in a sustained relationship have difficult childhoods, the interaction pattern in a marriage gets to be a bouillabaisse of blending flavors:

> "Am I mad at you because you are behaving like your crazy mom, or is the problem really me, because I'm responding like my angry dad? Or is it really both of us? Or do I really care? Maybe I should just leave. No, that's an old script I learned from my dad; he always cut out when the going got tough. But then, I must be crazy to stay with you. Oops, that's what my mom would say."

You get the picture. So that's the way it was with Sally and Harold. It can be a little confusing to sort out. Freud said that there are four people in every marriage bed. That was in days of few divorces and few stepchildren. Now there's an extended family of stepparents dancing through the minds and dreams of couples under the sheets.

However, I was able to help Sally and Harold each acknowledge the relationship melody that they had both learned in their childhoods. And after six weeks of work, the discordant noise became a passable harmony. I was happy for them, and pleased with the work they did. Harold, in therapy, worked through problems with his demanding mom. That helped him see Sally more realistically. Sally gave her alcoholic and abusive father at least a temporary boot out of her cortex, and could then see Harold as less demanding and controlling. Both departed from my time with them hand in hand, all kissy face.

It was about a year later that Sally called again. She was wading through a quagmire of anger and self-pity. Over the phone she kicked up several buckets of swamp water all over my end of the receiver. She almost breathlessly described in some detail how Harold had deteriorated since they had last seen me. I urged her to make an appointment for them both, as she clarified that they were ready "to hit the road in separate directions again."

The following weekend, we had a marathon session for three hours, filled with remonstrations, anger, tears, and renewed affection. Holding each other and weeping, the swamp was drained a bit and filled in with a meadow of love. They redefined their relationship with an increased understanding of the other's point of view. I saw them three times for follow-up over the next six weeks, and I have to say they both continued to work hard, making a credible effort to overcome their natural tendencies of discounting the other. Always they left each session pretty much hand in hand. And I ended those sessions with warm feelings of real accomplishment.

I didn't hear from this couple again for perhaps three years. Then Sally phoned and said she was having some problems with Danny, their second child. We set up an appointment, and she and Danny waltzed in and not seeing Harold, I asked how the marriage was progressing.

She responded, "Oh, Harold and I are divorced."

"What?!" My surprise must have leaked through the old professional demeanor.

I was stunned, but before I could recover, Sally forged ahead with her old bulldozer finesse: "Foster, I think if Harold and I had gone to *any other* therapist who wasn't so darn effective and didn't believe so strongly that problems can always be worked through in a marriage, I would have been happily divorced long ago. I figure you slowed down my life by about two years or more."

I stammered out some super therapeutic responsive like, "Oh."

I thought long and hard about what she said. Unbidden at night, I would see Sally's slightly irritable face. And I thought about how personal beliefs *could have* contaminated therapy. I ruminated about those old professors warning about it years earlier. Heck, maybe I slowed Harold's life down two years too! After all, Sally wasn't the picture of an easygoing wife! And the more I thought about it, the more I realized that my sweet wife, Hermie, and I had been through a lot of ups and downs in our marriage. Hard times and great times. And through it all, we always knew that *we* could work out anything within *our* relationship. Had that experience slopped over to my couple counseling? Possibly. Well, let's be honest! Not possibly, probably!

So ever after, when I saw jealous, spitting, and fussing couples I clarified, up front, that I generally believed almost anything could be worked through with effort, good guidance, and good will within a marital relationship. I explained that this belief was a *bias* of mine and that I would try to keep it ever in my awareness and under control. However, I explained, I had not always been aware of that bias and I would, by way of explanation, sometimes tell this story, just as I have told it here—how one lady thought I had slowed down her life for two years and helped me be aware of how personal history can affect therapy.

8. AN ELEVATOR RIDE WITH WOLF MAN

"Wolf Man." That's what he was called. He was a legend around the psych unit at the Seattle VA Hospital. Wolf Man. It wasn't used as a pejorative term; it was just a descriptor. These days it would be considered politically inappropriate to give patients pet names. But in bygone days, patients had pet names for staff, and staff had pet names for some patients. His given name was Gene Walton, and he was ordinarily a very big and quiet man. He might impress one as a little standoffish. Most wouldn't choose him as a best friend, but I'm sure some could happily go shopping with him. He would impress most of us as "Mr. Cellophane." *He could stand right there and you'd never ask his name.* He was quiet, marginally responsive, but certainly not animated.

Not everyone need be a pool of animated fun. Mr. Walton was pleasant in a distant sort of way. Much of the time, when on the unit, he would sit around reading or quietly conversing with a little fixed smile on his face. His eyes may not have been inviting and perhaps four clicks short of friendly, but they weren't downright menacing, either.

On medication, most who suffer from psychotic breaks don't continually live "around the bend," but they often hear out-of-sight whispers calling them to them. That whispering call often tells them not to take the very medication that keeps the whispers from becoming a shout. Certainly some prefer to travel around the bend openly rageful, rather than attempt to cope sanely with the everyday world of intimacy, pain, and problems. Perhaps that was true of Mr. Walton. He could never really clarify why he would quit his meds.

When Mr. Walton was off his medication—watch out!

On first starting my training on the psychiatric floor at the VA hospital, I heard that in his rage, Mr. Walton had been known to bite people. But worse than the bite were the guttural growls that would rumble up from God knows where. It was the growls more than the biting that gave him his name. Would he actually eat someone like a wolf might gobble someone down? Of course not! But he was plenty able to hurt someone seriously. Mr. Walton was a very big man. At 6'2" he weighed in at about 250 pounds.

Mr. Walton seemed to quit his medication every six months or so. There was speculation that Mrs. Walton's constant nagging could drive anyone to run around the bend, and if you lived with her, you'd be willing to travel that road too. But I'm not so sure. Maybe that was unfair to her. I don't know if any homeport could ever be as painful as the place Mr. Walton ran to when off medication. Most people would choose quite a bit of domestic pain rather than walk off onto Mr. Walton's path.

Some of the vets at the VA would play their "I-am-a-mental-health-psycho" drama to insure the continuation of the many perks offered by the VA system. But we never felt that way about Mr. Walton. He was a bonafide. He deserved every pill ever prescribed for him.

Mr. Walton was a Viet Nam vet who had lived through the fighting in the Ming Kong Delta, and it left him scarred. On the psychiatric unit, more than once, he had awakened screaming. He said that at night images of people he'd either killed or buddies he'd seen die crept from the caves of his mind and came out to play. He said with a very flat effect that he'd killed some folks who didn't deserve to die. I wondered if he continued to be threatening as a way of insuring punishment. I speculated about this with him but to no avail. Phenothiazines, indeed almost any good antipsychotic, would keep his bad guys locked up at least temporarily. They weren't so troublesome during the daylight hours. But at night it was more difficult to keep the ghosts at bay. At those times, Mr. Walton would shuffle out to the nurse's station frightened, whites of his eyes showing, and apologetically ask in his flat voice, "I hate to bother you, ma'am, but can I just sit here by the station for a while?"

And if there was no anger mixed with the terror in those eyes, the nurses felt comfortable having him sit there in the hall like a statue outside the station. There he might be seen at all hours of the night.

But if there was rage in his corner-of-the-eye-glint, the charge nurse would reach out and punch one of the six buttons on the old black telephone while saying, "Mr. Walton, I'd be more comfortable if you waited in your room and I'll get the doctor to talk with you."

That could mean real trouble for the physicians, because on a couple of infamous occasions Mr. Walton had actually attacked them. The night would then be filled with the guttural utterings of the Wolf Man growling in his restraints before a tranquilizer would shove away the demons and float Mr. Walton out of his misery.

Mr. Walton would be admitted for about a week when he needed his medications regulated. As I said, for reasons known only to Mr. Walton, he fairly reliably quit taking his meds every six months following discharge. Most of us residents might never meet him, but we knew of him. We knew of his reputation for possible violence. When we talked about the rare event of being attacked by a patient, we even called it being "Waltonized"

41

in awed commemoration of Mr. Walton's more memorable moments.

There. Now you know what I knew when the call came in. Janice requested me in the emergency room. "Foster, the Waltons are here."

It wasn't late in the evening. That was nice. I was up on the psych unit on the eighth floor at the time. This simple call caused a bit of flurry behind the desk. The charge nurse asked, "Can you get the help ready if you need it?"

She started fluttering around, unlocking the meds cabinet, bobbing her head like a little bird as she more than obviously checked out its contents.

"Sure," I responded.

All this activity might have been for show, or for real, or for both. I thought the two night staff nurses might have been half kidding. However, their banging around in the med cabinet was a little unsettling to me. These ladies knew Mr. Walton and I had never met him.

When I arrived in admissions, Mrs. Walton was sitting outside the exam cubicle. Most husbands and wives stayed together inside the green curtains. Evidently one of them didn't want to be with the other. Maybe it was a mutual decision.

Mrs. Walton was a small graying lady. She said quietly, "Gene is having a hard time and I thought I'd better bring him in." That was when I heard the heavy breathing issuing from behind the curtains of the exam cubicle. It was as if, upon hearing his wife's voice talking to some professional, Mr. Walton took his cue to start huffing like a steam engine making for the summit of a long, steep grade.

I peeked through the curtains. Mr. Walton was sitting on the exam table hunched over, drooling on his leg and breathing really, really hard. It wasn't heavy breathing like someone who might be having a heart attack. It was more like the heavy breathing of a big bear looking down at the deer he'd just killed.

"Well, okay, let's get moving on this."

Usually I fill out paperwork and interview in the admission area. This time it seemed that the better part of valor was to hustle Mr. Walton right on up to the eighth floor.

So I, myself, hurried right out to the desk and asked Janice for the male aides to accompany me up to the unit with Mr. Walton.

"Sorry, Dr. Cline, they're helping with a couple who were in a car accident." The accident had occurred about half an hour earlier and the aides were trying to comfort a weeping wife while she waited for completion of her husband's x-rays. Well, that was just peachy keen. Everything breaks loose at once doesn't it? Mr. Walton couldn't wait. I thought about interrupting the aides and the crying wife, but that seemed terribly rude and intrusive.

I said to the admissions clerk, "Well, call Jack Nichols to meet me down here." Jack Nichols was the surgical resident on call. We had gone through medical school together. He was big.

"Dr. Nichols is up in Op 4 with a ruptured appy." Okay, so he was in the operating room helping with an appendectomy.

"Who's the medical on call?"

"Dorothy Jeffers, but she's busy in x-ray."

"Oh." I wanted a male on call anyway. I didn't realize it was Dorothy's rotation.

At this point I slid from concerned into low-grade desperate.

"Well, who's around to help me get Mr. Walton up to the unit?"

"Not a soul that I can think of, Dr. Cline," which meant, "Buddy, it's not in *our* job description, that's for sure."

This unhappy conversation didn't take long. So I ambled back to the cubicle wondering what to do. Mr. Walton's boiler was getting up a heavier head of steam. His breathing was a little deeper. Not good. I had the definite feeling that if I said, "Mr. Walton, I'm going to give you a little shot to help you relax," all hell would break loose. He really didn't look like he was into relaxing. So he could either sit there in a basically empty admissions area, with the pressure building, heading toward eruption, or I could get him up on the unit, where the staff was hopefully ready and waiting with a tranquilizer if needed.

"Mr. Walton, I'd like to go up to the unit with you."

Mr. Walton rose to his feet and started heading the opening in the green curtains of the cubicle. I was about to ask Mrs. Walton to come along but she anticipated me and shook her head quite firmly and with genuine fright, "No!" She obviously didn't want any part of the ride up to the eighth floor. This was not good. Maybe I ought to rethink my plan. However, by this point Mr. Walton was shuffling right along down the hall, like a horse heading home to the barn.

This perhaps was good. He was cooperative. This would probably work out. The hall was deserted as we waited for the elevator.

Now I must digress and explain the VA elevators. Did you know that the cost of an elevator is based on the size and speed of the motor, not on how high the elevator goes? Speed costs money. The VA system saved *massive amounts* on its elevators. They literally crept. It was a standing laughable truth that staff could hop up the stairs on one foot and beat the elevators. So we waited quite a while on the first floor. A black couple, perhaps the family of the man in the surgical suite, walked up to take the elevator. The sight of Mr. Walton, standing there hunched over, still drooling, with his guttural breathing, helped them to reconsider. They evidently decided that they really needed the exercise. Throwing me glances of mixed fright, concern, and compassion, they made for the stairs.

Finally, the elevator arrived. Mr. Walton and I got on. He leaned against a back corner breathing even deeper by this time. I stayed up front near the control panel. I think I hoped that if I stared at the panel, as well as keying it forcefully, the elevator might hurry just a bit. The eighth floor door opening needed to be activated with a brass key. Turning the key forcefully with my sweaty fingers didn't seem to encourage the doors to slide close faster here on the first floor. The elevator in the VA was designed to stop right in the middle of the eighth floor psych unit. That, among other reasons, is why access to the floor was locked. I continued to concentrate on the key and turn it with silent zeal.

Slowly the doors sighed closed and the elevator shuddered and started its grind up. This was good. At ten seconds a floor, we had just over a minute.

To my surprise, the elevator ground to an almost imperceptible stop on third, the x-ray and lab floor. The doors slowly and ponderously slid opened. Before I could think to warn anyone that this really should be a private trip, Dorothy, the medical on call, backed in a wheelchair patient. Wheelchairs are always backed into elevators because those little front swivel wheels don't like elevator floor sills. Without even giving us a glance, poor Dorothy backed in, almost touching Mr. Walton who now, standing kitty-corner behind her, had his eyes fixed down on the head of this guy in the wheel chair. As the doors closed, I think she heard the breathing. Who couldn't? I could see her back stiffen just a bit, but it was too late.

The patient was evidently the husband of the weeping woman in the ER. His head, wrapped in white gauze, had a big red splotch of blood leaking through the occiput. He was real still and facing the door.

Mr. Walton slowly looked closer and leaned forward, still drooling, his

44

eyes fixed on the blood spot. He reminded me of a crow and if crows could pounce on carrion, he was ready to pounce. He started breathing much more deeply with an ominous little feeding puff at the end of each exhale. By this time, Dorothy was way, way too scared to turn around, but she reached out and pushed the button for the fourth floor. Was that the intended original destination—the closed-for-the-night doctor and nurses' lounges? I doubted it very much. There were no beds on fourth floor. But this was a bright lady and, without looking, she wanted *off this elevator now!*

The guy in the wheelchair didn't look around either. He remained rigid. I think that while Mr. Walton was breathing heavier, this poor guy was literally holding his breath. I decided to say something to perhaps cover the breathing. As if I'm Dr. Congenial, I said, "Oh, hi, Dorothy. You're getting off on four?" Perhaps I said it to give Mr. Walton some hope that he only needed to hold off a possible feeding frenzy for one more floor. Dorothy, maintaining her wonderful sense of humor, answered without looking around, "Three and a half, if possible."

The elevator hesitated imperceptibly and sighed to a stop on four. Dorothy scraped that wheel chair right through the doors before they even finished opening. Then they ponderously closed, leaving me alone with Mr. Walton. I wanted to say something terrifically helpful. But my brain wasn't sparking, so I heard myself inanely saying "Well, Mr. Walton nice to have you back," or something super stupid like that. My comment caused him to breathe harder. A psychiatrist who could only think to say something like that must not have provided much reassurance.

The elevator crawled up the shaft. The only thing that marked the passage of time was Mr. Walton's increasingly audible expiratory growl. I was thinking of how to best defend myself with my bare hands but was totally clueless. When the elevator finally stopped and the doors inched open on the eighth floor, two young night watchmen were standing right there with the two night nurses, waiting for our arrival.

Janice must have called up from admissions and warned the floor staff. And they had called security. Mr. Walton, on the opening of that door, felt it safe to blow.

I've found that many people intuitively think that if folks are really angry and violent, it might well take a football team to restrain and contain them. But it doesn't. Five is more than enough.

Within an hour Mr. Walton was snoozing with a barbiturate, traveling around the bend far away from his demons. A very relieved young physician was thinking, "If I have a spare minute this week, I really ought to write this one up!"

9. FEDERAL ECONOMICS 101

Most veterans are thoughtful men who have been through tough situations. And most cope exceedingly well with their experiences. Some who have experienced combat deal with PTSD, the psychological result of war trauma. These men deserve our thanks, as well as our compassion, understanding, and support. Lately the Veterans Hospital has come in for much criticism for providing less than optimal care. However, in the seventies, when this story took place, the VA provided very good care. The psychiatric units of the nation's VA hospitals were filled with caregivers, from doctors, occupational therapists (OTs), social workers, and psychologists, right down to the caring young female candy stripers. All were compassionate folks.

Admission, of course, was an earned benefit, and life on the unit was basically good. With many more benefits than simply free board and room, there were some vets who understandably tended to play the system. Therefore the following essay of an experience I had in the seventies should by no means reflect poorly on the thousands of young Americans who have served and given their best, often their lives and limbs, in the service of our country.

I looked forward to the VA rotation part of my training, perhaps partially because it paid so well. The good old government was as generous to the professionals as it was to the veterans in those days. The average taxpayer has no idea how generous he is! Taxpayers were certainly generous to us! The pay at the VA was nearly double what we received at the county and university hospitals (which was barely enough to pay for food and rent). We soon came to appreciatively call the VA "the Vaa."(It rhymes with "baa.")

In the late sixties and early seventies, the Vaas were totally win/win situations. Win for the docs. Win for the patients. As mentioned, the Vaa doctors were paid very well, indeed. Even all of us lowly residents in training were paid nicely. However, the big winners in those days were the psychiatric patients. The only folks who lost were the taxpayers, who paid very handsomely indeed into this sprawling self-serving bureaucracy.

The psych units were pleasant and caring places to hang out. And the few vets who really took unfair advantage of the system were referred to by the staff as "gomers."

The gomers hit the jackpot on admission, because hanging out at the Vaa brought many benefits indeed. First was the phenomenal pay. Most gomers, some of whom had obviously manipulated to get a disability in the first place, parlayed their small disability into hundreds of dollars a month. For instance, we had Eric Gomer up on the unit. Eric had managed to shoot himself in the foot in Viet Nam and had been awarded a 10 percent disability. That allowed him to flee Viet Nam while others remained in dangerous situations. Eric Gomer (supposedly) suffered for years, filled with inconsolable guilt over that bug out. Other gomers might have slight visual or hearing disabilities that caused unending and unendurable anxiety. Years after their service, many continued to claim stress and anxiety. But somehow, in spite of all the help and understanding, therapy and effort, they just couldn't work it through.

It really didn't matter how small or what their disability might be, because whatever percent disability they had managed to eek out of the system, it became a roaring bonanza on admission to the VA hospitals, because *all* disabilities immediately jumped to 100 percent.

The government, in its wisdom, concluded that by the very nature of an admission itself, anyone admitted to a VA hospital *had* to "earn" a 100 percent disability during their hospitalization. And since all care to veterans was absolutely free, vets could do very well collecting that 100 percent disability. Over a summer they could sock away hundreds, if not thousands, of dollars. And in winter, when Seattle was damp and rainy, the hospitals in sunny California would still be there waiting for them.

Following close on the heels of the money benefit was attention given by gaggles of pretty, all-caring, all-eager, all-gullible nursing students. Following the nurses closely in gomer preference were the young and impressionable high school Candy Stripers, and there were bevies of nurse's aides and young OTs. Embryonic professionals rotated through the VA before going out into practice: physicians, OTs, registered and licensed nurses, nurse aides, and social workers. The vets who took advantage of this situation easily manipulated the young naïve hatchlings in all sorts of ways I need not go into here. Let your imagination run wild! They went through the Vaa nest like wolves through a hen house.

But there was more enjoyment for these guys than simply manipulating the personnel. Physically, the Seattle Vaa was a nice place to hang out. Situated on one of the highest hills in the city, it had a commanding view of Elliot Bay. The lawn, like all federal greenways, was beautifully manicured. The food was excellent. When one considers the pay, the board and room, and the nursing attention, it was a most comfortable resort. And if some refused to work on their problems and didn't seem to improve at all, that meant they obviously needed an even longer stay.

48

When first arriving at the Vaa, having been at the county and university hospitals, I only looked forward to the increase in my monthly stipend. I didn't realize how the Vaa was simply another example of the *Great-Federal-Feeding-Trough*. My education into Fed economics happened like this:

On my first day, the head nurse showed me around the ward. "Dr. Cline, this is the unit," explained "Nurse Ratchet." She was big. She was mighty. Everyone gave her great deference. The men that I later came to know as the gomers were sitting around the "Day Room" doing their "day thing." One could never figure out why it was called the Day Room, because the men played the same poker and cribbage at night. It was used as a library for reading, playing checkers, watching TV, and keeping the popcorn machine warmed up. Watching TV was by far the most popular day occupation. Smoking, of course, was allowed. Heck, in those days the vets were given free cigarettes. So Ratchet and I walked through a cloud of smoke into the Day Room.

Even the gomers were respectful to Louise Ratchet. They answered her with "Yes, ma'ams" when addressed. It was a different story when I made my first rounds the next morning. The gomers broke in the new doc with nothing but complaints. I use their exact language at this point, and will perhaps remove it with final editing.

"The f...ing food here will make you sick." Or, "The f...ing nurses don't give a damn about what kind of care a person receives." A common gomer complaint was not getting the f...ing pass they deserved. The basic complaint was that the f...ing hospital hadn't helped them one bit. For the first days, I took the complaints most seriously and my feelings were hurt when staff laughed at my gullibility. And I soon learned that the true gomers had absolutely no investment in "getting better," whatever the heck that meant!

They missed appointments, they kissed off group meetings, and mostly they were true experts in the blame and complaint departments. It only took a day or so for them to realize that even I, their all-caring young resident physician, "didn't really give a f..." about them. I'll drop the language now. You get the idea. Just be assured that sexual exclamations were ubiquitous. All nurses were female dogs, and most males never had fathers.

I'm a slow learner, but by the end of the second week even I got the picture. On the memorable morning of the third week, I buzzed through the unit on morning rounds and shocked all with a new agenda.

When the first gomer said, "Damn it, doc, I've been here ten weeks and this f...ing place hasn't helped me a bit." I replied, "You know what, Eddie? I appreciate your candor. And you are *so* right. We've done about the best we can, and you haven't been helped a bit. Since we can't do much better or differently, I'm discharging you today."

This was the first time I saw *real* anger bordering on shocked rage behind the oily whines that had been so common. *"What! What the f... is wrong with you? You can't do that! You can't just say that I'm outta here."*

"I just did, Ed. You are out!"

That morning I discharged most of the day room poker club. Out with every one! That very morning, six charts read, with a slight flourish:

"Discharge today. Foster W. Cline, M.D."

I always left the charts with new orders on the counter. On completing my rounds, I found Ratchet flipping through the charts. She looked almost horrified. That surprised me. Her eyes were like saucers. It was the first time in my three weeks that I saw Louise look downright worried. I didn't think she was capable of worry.

"Foster, you can't really do that."

I smiled reassuringly. I had read my job description. Chief Resident Physician. Not to worry, Eleanor. "Not only can I, I just did. Admissions and discharge are my prerogatives while I'm on this unit. Look, Eleanor, you know the situation. These guys are here for three hot meals a day. We have babysat these guys long enough, right? They've been sitting around doing little to nothing for weeks. Most for months. They're outta here."

Eleanor smiled. Was there a tad of pity for me in those eyes? That couldn't be, could it? "You are of course right, *doctor.* But you still shouldn't have done it." The way she said *"doctor"* made me feel a bit disconcerted and vexed. Her words were an unhappy blend of sarcasm mixed with a dash of sorrow.

After writing some other orders for passes, sleep medication, and miscellaneous medical problems, I checked my schedule for the day and walked off the unit to get coffee in the basement cafeteria. Did I feel a little proud of myself? I have to admit that I did. I had saved the taxpayers a swimming pool of bucks!

The very next day, I found that my decision was about to be recognized, validated, and appreciated. In fact, I received an invitation to see Colonel Big himself down in the administration inner sanctum. He had invited me down at 2:00 to his plush digs on the first floor. Colonel Big was the hospital administrator. He was a huge man with a punched-in nose and a flat face. A surgeon by training, he always walked around with a white lab coat and a stethoscope stretched around his pudgy neck. He was respected as an able administrator, albeit with poor people skills. And that didn't matter one iota, because with his rank as head of the Seattle Vaa, who needed to mess with people skills!

Dr. Big didn't keep me waiting, and the secretary said I could go right in. Was there a hint of irritation in his face? How could that be? I had just saved the Veterans Administration and the American Taxpayers $900 per day per gomer. And that was only the cost of hospitalization. These guys were collecting their 100 percent disability of about $200 per day on top of that. Let's see…. I figured I was saving the hospital and the American taxpayers at least $1,000 per gomer per day. Times 6 gomers discharged, that works out to be about $180,000 gomer bucks a month. A very tidy sum indeed!

Dr. Big met me with a smile and a handshake. He asked me if I wanted to sit down and I plopped right into one of his big leather easy chairs. Then he started the preamble to his commendation. "Dr. Cline, did you discharge six patients yesterday?"

"I did," I proudly said.

"That's more or less a record," said Dr. Big, still smiling broadly.

I happily thought, "Aw, shucks, it was nothing really. Why didn't the previous physicians do it?" Of course I was bright enough not to say that, but I did grin and demurely mutter my "Thanks."

Still smiling, he asked me if I liked my VA pay. Hmmm. Where was this going? Like the pay…? Heck no, I loved it! "Yeah," I admitted a little hesitantly. "It's pretty darn good pay." Just then it occurred to me that Colonel Big's smile had a slightly immobile quality, much as if, with difficulty, he had it pasted on.

He asked, still smiling a little too broadly, "Do you know how our pay is figured?"

"No, not really." I felt like the *Titanic*. I had been the greatest ship in the world. Now with Dr. Big's white coat towering over me, I sensed an iceberg ahead.

Colonel Big came out of his chair. His smile had somehow disappeared into a completely red face. He walked around his desk toward me. Was I intimidated? Not a bit. I was terrorized. He shouted, "BED OCCUPANCY. DAMN IT, CLINE, OUR PAY IS FIGURED BY BED OCCUPANCY!"

The *Titanic* just hit the iceberg.

"Do not, I repeat, DO NOT *EVER* DISCARGE A VA PATIENT UNLESS YOU HAVE SOMEONE ELSE TO FILL THAT BED THAT DAY. AM I MAKING MYSELF ABSOLUTELY CLEAR!?" The *Titanic* was now busted in half and spiraling down to the ocean bottom. This man was not mad, he was absolutely furious.

I sat there for a moment in silence, and then stumbled into a hesitant, squeaky voice that struggled through a collapsed larynx. "I like the pay, but these six guys were costing the taxpayers about $180,000 a month. Nothing was being accomplished. They were working the system, Dr. Big. There's a problem with the system."

I think Dr. Big was dumbstruck that anyone would answer him so directly. He sat down in his chair. There was a long period of silence. Then he said quietly, very quietly, because he was keeping himself under control. "Dr. Cline, people like you have only three choices in life. First, you can climb the ladder of promotion in our system, and reach a rank high enough to change the system. In your case, that would appear to me highly unlikely. Secondly, you can bitch and moan from within the system and change nothing. You might be good at that. Thirdly, you can go out and start your own system and run it however the hell you want. Will you remember this, Dr. Cline?"

Gosh, yes! I've never forgotten that advice. I nodded. Dr. Big stood up. The interview was over. He gave me a tight little smile and held out his big meaty hand. I reached out, thinking there was a good chance he would try to crush my metacarpals. But surprisingly, his shake was firm and warm. He looked almost warmly into my eyes—perhaps it was pity. At any rate, he shocked me by saying sincerely, "Good luck, Dr. Cline."

Over the years, Colonel Big's words have often rattled through my cortex unbidden. I think about those words and I think about the thirty years that I took them to heart while starting and building my own clinic. For those thirty years I worked with a boss (me) that made some mistakes. But he never made me attend a meeting that was boring or unnecessary. He tried very hard NOT to waste anyone's time or money. He didn't treat people who didn't need to be treated. And although, at many times, he worked me like a son of a bitch, I never disagreed with even one of his decisions.

10. JANET YANKED THAT KID
RIGHT OUT OF THE CAR

The light blue new Cadillac came screeching to a stop in the driveway of a beautiful mega home. With a fiery red face, Janet Anderson popped out of the driver's door, ran around the front of her new Caddie, and jerked open the opposite back door. She grabbed eight-year-old Jake's right arm, yanking the protesting boy right out of the car. With a voice that would freeze alcohol she said, "Okay, young man, I don't know exactly what is going to happen to you for what you've done, but when your father finishes with you, you won't like it!"

This is a story of how Jake showed his parents that an eight-year-old can rule the house!

Janet was normally a fairly laid back person. But her first experience parenting a foster child had rocketed her far beyond frustration right over the event horizon to spiral into complete distraction. In the previous counseling session, she had wailed, "It is like this eight-year-old kid is out to get me!"

Before continuing with this unhappy tale, background is important. Foster parents are the unsung heroes in a nation that produces thousands of abused and neglected children every year. Our national social policies are apparently designed to encourage marginally functional single parents to produce an ever-increasing litter of uncared for or abused children. These children in turn feed a burgeoning and ever-increasing federal and state funded social service system—a system where abused and neglected children provide employment opportunities for judges, parole officers, police, child advocates, social service personnel, child care facilities and foster parents. The most poorly paid and unappreciated lot of the system's employment beneficiaries are the foster parents who are on duty 24 hours a day, seven days a week.

Americans unfamiliar with this system and the unhappy children who inhabit various aspects of the system understandably feel sorry for the "poor kids." Those familiar with the system consider the foster parents "saints" and mutter under their breath, "I sure couldn't handle most of those children!" There aren't many judges, probation officers, and social service employees who take these kids into their own homes, that's for sure!

Many, if not most, of the children placed in foster care come from homes where there has been an ongoing war between the adults and the kids. Prior to the Anderson foster home, Jake was removed from a typical dysfunctional family in which the battles were psychological, verbal, and often physical. Like many children who are removed from the birth parents, Jake was living with one parent and his mother's live-in partner, the latest in her long line of unsuccessful relationships. As the years pass, Jake and other children like him, understandably become experts at battle maneuvers with authority figures and with setting up and winning sieges of interpersonal manipulation. In many cases, it is this knowledge that has kept them alive.

A child who feels he or she is unlovable enters a foster home where parents proclaim, "We have so much love to share." On the surface, this may appear to be a perfect fit and it often ends up that way. But the path toward mutual respect and affection is uphill and rocky. These children have learned not to trust and have learned to survive only by grubbing off every inch of control they are able. Generally, they are not initially enjoyable or lovable children.

As Shakespeare noted, "All the world's a stage, and all the men and women merely players. They have their exits and their entrances." The problem is, the only play Jake knew was the one into which he had been born and bred. He had played only one part for his entire life. Humans, adults or children, are loath to change the play.

Jake's own lifelong script played out in a drama in which people mainly fight; where control is not shared, but demanded; where genuine love is absent; and where survival depends on being able to predict a future only if it is manipulated and managed. Jake's cup of tea was a home where the mom was mad at the kid. Where the parents fought with each other and where kids could lie their way out of tight spots.

When Jake entered a home with authority figures who only wanted to show love, there was a complete disconnect. Jake could only feel helpless. From experience, helplessness led to pain and had to be avoided at almost all costs. It had never made sense to try to love a mother. And when a mother said she loved him, it was only to feed her own bottomless needs. And besides that, there was no honesty from anyone, anyway!

From Jake's point of view, Janet and Ned Anderson definitely needed to learn their parts in the playbook he owned—a playbook where a smart eight-year-old could predict and even manipulate adult fights; where the primary adult emotion was frustration and the primary child response was anger, lying, cheating, resentment, and disobedience. That was the home he knew and a home that he could cope with!

Perhaps deep in his soul, Jake felt a certain satisfaction in mentoring his new parents as they learned their part in his play. This story is about one of many early episodes in which Jake helped his parents audition for their new roles.

Janet had made the mistake of taking Jake shopping without any contract for what would be bought or a contract for behavioral expectations. She had compounded that mistake by refusing, after shopping, to stop for a McDonald's shake just because "Jake had acted like a complete out-of-control and disrespectful ass" throughout their entire shopping trip at the mall.

On driving home, Janet told Jake she was not stopping for a McDonald's shake. Jake started yelling from the back seat, in a long, obnoxious and loud singsong: "You never want to do anything I want to. You always say, 'no' no matter what! You just hate me." Foolish Janet, not yet knowing her part in his drama script, responded, "I don't hate you, but I don't like the way you act." Jake must have wondered, "What kind of response is that!?" It was far too rational. It was not a known part of his known universe of parenting!

So Jake escalated to an unending, "I hate you, I hate you." This led to a frustrated "You stop that right now" from Janet. This unenforceable demand was Jake's cup of tea. He felt right at home now. Although, from Jake's point of view, frustrated, unenforceable demands were a definite improvement, Janet was not yet at the point of complete emotional collapse, the endpoint to which Jake had led all other mothers. Something a lot more creative was called for.

As Janet spied the reflection of her son in the rearview mirror, she saw him raise a pencil and bring it down hard punching a hole in the back seat of her new car. She took a microsecond to berate herself for leaving her purse in the backseat where Jake could find the pencil. But that moment of self-reproach was fleeting, as she was overwhelmed with rage as she heard the holes being punched in the back seat of her new blue caddie.

"I hate you!" Up came the pencil in the rearview mirror. Down went the pencil with a thud into the upholstery of the seat. "I hate you." Up came the pencil. Down it went, time after time, in the rearview mirror. Obviously, this young incorrigible was doing all he could to ventilate the seat cushion in a car already air-conditioned. As they were already in the home neighborhood, and inevitable and severe damage had already taken place, stopping the car did not seem like a viable option. Besides, Janet could only keep herself under minimal control by repeating, "I must get home, I must get home, I must get home."

As the car skidded to a stop, Janet bounded out, sprinted around the back, threw open the door, and yanked Jake out of the car, knowing that if she even glanced at the ruined seat, she was in danger of strangling the son she had promised social services that she would love. Hardly able to speak, she made the pronouncement concerning Jake's unhappy future as she envisioned her husband imposing consequences just short of Jake's death.

As she dragged Jake up the walk to the beautifully inlaid front door, he continued to screech, in a perfect example of self-fulfillment, "You hate me! You hate me!"

Ned Anderson was home and hearing the mayhem he opened the door to see his silent fiery wife and a son whose yelling approached the limit of the neighborhood's noise covenants. "Gees! What's the problem!?" he asked.

"It's Jake," started Janet, just short of a shriek herself. "He just punched holes all over the backseat of the new car!"

Jake, amidst tears, appealed to his father, "I did not! She lies. She always lies about me! She hates me."

Ned said, almost firmly, "Jake, did you punch holes in the back seat?"

This question did not sit at all well with Janet who, with eyes snapping, snarled, "Ned, I just told you that he punched holes in the car. You don't have to ask him!"

However, not taking advantage of any parental intermission, Jake continued to wail, "I didn't punch one hole! She's just saying that to make you mad at me. She always lies about me."

Ned, now feeling caught in the middle, said, "Janet, you and I don't have to fight about this. I can just go to the car and look. We can check it out."

This response, Janet knew, was typical milk toast Ned. And it tipped Janet over the edge of complete apoplexy. Now, seething, with indignant impotent rage, and outshouting Jake by several decibels, she fairly screamed at her husband, "Dammit, Ned, make up your mind. Who you are going to believe!? Me or this kid?"

All this was said in the midst of Jake continuing to plead, "Dad, please just believe me. Just look. That's all I ask. Just look. She always hates me and tries to get me in trouble."

Unfortunately, this plea pulled a bit at Ned's frayed heartstrings. Lately, he had actually wondered if Janet had been picking on Jake. Of course, this had surprised him because she had always been so good with children. But ever since Jake had come into the house, he had wondered if, in regards to Jake, his angel wife was turning into a witch. "Honey," he said, almost apologetically, "I'm going to go check. This is easy enough to sort out."

Janet exploded, "FINE!"—which is many a woman's way of saying, "Go ahead and do it, but at your own risk."

Jake reached out and took his father's hand. "Thanks, Dad." This little interaction almost pushed Janet even further over the edge, but she held her tongue as Jake and her husband ambled along the walkway, hand in hand, to the car. Ned opened the back door.

Shocked, devastated, and with disbelief, she heard Jake proclaim with a satisfied vindication, "There, Dad, you see? She hates me."

"Janet," Ned called, "I don't see any holes."

What?! How can this be? Head spinning, Janet, feeling she has just tripped into the twilight zone, walks rigidly to the car and sees…a perfectly beautiful back seat.

Stunned, Janet whispers, "But how can this be?" At the same time, she is parboiled with the knowledge that she has been absolutely outwitted and played for a sucker by this eight-year-old foster kid. She doesn't know how he did it, but he did. She is helplessly infuriated with Ned who now looks at her as if he's peering over the edge of sanity trying to find his wife. He has compassion in his eyes. How, he wonders, could Janet be making these things up? Maybe she needs to see a therapist herself. Maybe Dr. Cline ought to concentrate on fixing Janet, not Jake.

This kind of manipulation can stress the foundations of a good marriage. For the next two days until I saw this couple, Janet continued to maintain, to a disbelieving husband, that she was absolutely sure she had seen Jake poke holes in the seat of the car. Jake, for his part, ramped up the whole situation by a continual shuffle through the home, appearing hangdog and misunderstood in front of his dad, while shooting furtive eye-arrows at his mother.

Two days later, in a confrontational session in my office, Jake, taking a pencil, showed how he had pulled it off. He demonstrated how he could raise his fist so it would show in the rearview mirror, with the pencil pointing like a dagger down toward the seat. Then he revealed how, as his fist hit the seat, he loosened his grip on the pencil, which slid up harmlessly, while his blow made a satisfying thump on the seat, sounding for all the world as if a hole were being punched.

"But why would you do this?" asked an uncomprehending Ned Anderson.

"Because I hate Mom," answers his tearful son.

57

"But why?" persists his new father.

"I don't know," wails the eight-year-old as he bursts into tears. And mom and dad hug him together, and they are weeping too, and after a bit, after we talk about how these things happen, all three stand and leave, hand in hand, to continue up the rocky path toward love and mutual respect.

11. YOU REALLY SHOULD DIE IF FOLKS ARE
PRACTICING FOR YOUR FUNERAL

Some of the interesting folks we run into in life are not always the clients we see, but other professionals with whom we relate. It is well known that many with problematic backgrounds are drawn to work in the health field, especially the mental health field. As these reminiscences concern interesting people, Joyce Smith, a registered nurse, appears to qualify to be included here.

Joyce was about to kick the bucket. I first found that out when I was approached by Elaine Erickson, R.N., the director of education at The Willows, a long-term care facility. Call it a nursing home. Joyce, the lady on death's door, was a practical nurse at the facility. At the time, I was medical director at The Willows and consulted there twice a month. It was not uncommon for a long-term care facility to have a psychiatrist as medical director when, because of mental hospital closures, many long-term care facilities had a youth wing filled with challenged younger people needing help coping with the activities of daily living. Also, many of the everyday challenges in a long-term care facility involve geriatric psychiatric issues.

One morning on my arrival, Elaine Erickson asked, "Would you please take time to see Joyce Smith today, Foster? She has a short time to live, and needs some support in helping her extended family in California prepare for her passing. She asked to talk to you."

The thirtyish woman was waiting for me in the consultation room. She had a round not unpleasant face and was spiffy in her nurses' aide uniform. After a mutual greeting, she said, "I have a niece in California." Then she continued to explain, "I have not seen my niece in many years, and we have been estranged and angry with each other. But when she was a child, she loved her auntie." Tears now glistened in Joyce's eyes. "I just don't know how to tell her about...about...about...." It seemed obvious that she was struggling with her own passing and so was understandably uncertain how to discuss it with others.

When people are dying, they have one last gift to give others who will inevitably tread the same road. That gift is to show how to die well. If not welcoming the grim reaper, one can at least model how to look the old geezer in the eye and not flinch. Joyce could still teach her niece a bit. And she probably could die on good terms with her. I talked with her about this.

Joyce had let folks know that her diagnosis was severe polyarteritis, with likely vessel clampdown and circulatory collapse not far off in the future. I've seen many folks pausing before death's door following such a chronic illness, and the appearance of death is inevitably upon them. It shows in the look in their eyes, in the usual quiet acceptance that is often present in their voice. Sometimes there is a brave gallows humor. Joyce didn't have any of these signs and looked pretty much like she could continue to happily bounce down life's path. Her complexion was ruddy, and she had none of the shiny tightness to her skin so often present in peripheral vascular disease. To me on that day, she just looked too darn healthy.

Later, I said to Elaine Erickson, "She looks too well for someone knocking at death's door, don'tcha think? Are you all sure about the diagnosis?"

She hesitated. "Well, Foster, I've seen some lab results that have come through here with pretty high sedimentation rates," she said, her wide-eyed look at the mention of the lab results indicating that something was likely to be very wrong. "Her blood chemistry is way off." But I could see in her eyes that my question led Elaine to recognize a little niggle of doubt that might have been scrambling to claw its way into her own awareness. Joyce just didn't *look* all that sick.

A month passed.

Thoughts of Joyce Smith scooted away into the cracks of my cortex, far out of awareness until I received a call from the director of nurses at the Willows.

"Foster, this Ann Johnson. I'm phoning about Joyce…. She has missed a lot of work. I contacted her physician about what we should expect given the severity of her illness, and whether or not she would be completely bedridden as the end approached. He seemed shocked when I asked him about her illness and death. He wouldn't really talk to me. Actually, he said he *couldn't* talk to me. But I have a very bad feeling about all this. Will you phone him?"

"How has Joyce been doing?"

"Her hair has fallen out, and she has blue splotches on her skin. A little group of nurses is practicing her favorite hymns to sing at her funeral. Donna and Nancy went with her two days ago to the funeral home, and we have picked out a casket…. It was hard."

"What exactly did her doctor say?"

"Well, as I said, his reaction was one of shock. As I told him what Joyce has told us about her illness, he just kept muttering, 'What?! She said that?!'"

"What do you think about all this, Ann?"

"Darned if I know. I gotta say that doctor gave me the impression that everything I told him about Joyce's illness was news to him. But could she have made all this up? It's just too wacko, too bizarre. And her hair falling out, and the bluish areas of skin.... There's something going on."

Ann continued, "The staff here has been going to Joyce's home in the evening to sit with her at night, helping her through her night terrors. She had recently suffered one convulsion and bruised herself. She's been hospitalized for severe dehydration.... Gees, I don't know. Will you just please phone the physician and talk to him?"

I decided to hop on down to the facility and talk to Joyce first. Ann and I saw her together. Except for the fact that she was bald and had several blue and angry sores on her arms, she looked pretty healthy and perky to me. That afternoon, every unnecessary was filled with indignation when she learned the director of nursing had contacted her physician about her illness. She slammed into the office where Ann and I were talking and confronted Ann, saying, "That's just not right, that's just not right! It's none of your business. He's my doctor." As Joyce vibrated out her anger, Ann looked like she thought that Joyce was on the verge of attacking her. "How can you dare bother my physician and contact him about my illness, when it's only going to make me worse?! I'm already about to die as it is!"

I tried to explain to Joyce, to no avail, that Ann did what she had to do, as staffing was a problem and a schedule was needed for the following month. Joyce accused me of "being on Ann's side."

A schism was developing in the nursing staff. Some of the staff sympathized with Joyce and they huddled and whispered angry groups. How could Ann have been so nosey and uncaring? Others believed Ann had to phone because of staffing issues. People were taking sides.

After our visit, Ann again implored me to phone Joyce's physician, Dr. Knox, and receive straight information from him about Joyce's illness: "Come on, Foster, you guys can talk to each other doc to doc when I can't get anywhere with him." But I had patients to see for the remainder of the afternoon.

"Okay, I'll talk to him tomorrow when I'm normally here at the facility."

As I noted, twice a month I spent a full day at the Willows. And the next day was one of those monthly days. So in the morning I placed a call to Dr. Knox.

"I just can't tell you anything. I told that to your nurse. But I'll talk to my attorney today and find out what I can say. I'll phone you back."

About an hour later, Dr. Knox phoned me back and told me that on his attorney's advice, he could give me no information at all without a written release of information from Joyce Smith. He realized the problems I was having, sympathized with my position, and noted simply that he was legally unable to do and what he might professionally like to do. He left me with the strong impression that Joyce was not telling the truth, but at the same time, I had nothing to really confront her about. Staff polarization was continuing. Joyce had evidently phoned several friends and was continuing to "stir the brew" of the angry accusations toward Ann for making a direct inquiry to the doctor about of Joyce's illness.

That day, Joyce Smith was sick and not at work. Perhaps she didn't want to face me. She may have somehow intuited from the previous day's visit that I harbored some real doubts about her illness. She did leave me a note saying that although she was not able to come to work, her blood work was improving. Why not take the bull by the horns and phone Joyce Smith at home? With determination I dialed her number.

I didn't give Joyce time to think, argue, or hang up. I started out friendly, but forceful: "Hello, Joyce, this is Dr. Cline. I got the note you left for me today. It's good to know that your blood work is so much better and you are starting to have a remission." Okay, so much for the preamble. Now comes the kicker: "Nevertheless, Joyce, I need medical information from Dr. Knox about your illness and I want you to provide him with a written release for information about your illness."

There was dead silence on the other end of the line. After a few seconds of hesitation there was a slight gulping sound—"Whaaa...?"

Since Joyce was only gulping, I forged ahead. There was really no choice. I was forced into saying something. "Joyce, don't feel singled out by this. But it would be tacky if I, as medical director, were remiss in getting this information, just as you would want information about any aide who was ill if they were working with your patients. As medical director, I need to have this kind of information. I need his take on your prognosis and how long you can continue to work."

The other end of the line still sounded like it was hooked to deep space. Finally, in the distance, came a doubtful voice, "Well, I guess I'll give him a call."

"No, Joyce, that won't do it. I want you to go over to the clinic by two o'clock and sign the release. I'll probably be there about 2:15. I'll see you then."

"Whaaa…?"

"Really, Joyce, I expect to see you there, then."

Very hesitantly, she agreed. "Well…okay."

"Great! See you there."

After getting Joyce's reluctant agreement, I phoned Dr. Knox's secretary and told her that I would like to meet at 2:15 for a for few minutes and I expected that Joyce Smith would be there asking for a release for information.

At 1:45 John Branson, the director of the Willows, and I went over to the clinic and greeted the receptionist. I asked if Joyce had been in. She hadn't. "Well, I'm hoping that she'll be here shortly with a release of information." Doesn't hope bloom eternal? We waited until 2:30 and it was obvious Joyce wasn't going to show up.

I asked to see Dr. Knox anyway, and he came out—a nice, concerned and thoughtful-looking young man. I told him again that I simply wanted to meet him and that we were in a bind with Joyce. He somewhat hesitantly responded, "I understand where you are coming from Dr. Cline…and I truly wish I could help you…but without that release, my attorney says 'no way.' …But I guess I can say that I sure as heck would like a follow up on this one! Somebody has to work with this lady!"

I was about to leave the hospital/clinic complex when I decided it would be a good idea to phone Joyce Smith at home. After phoning The Willows and getting her number, we rang her up. No answer.

We knew she had been home earlier in the day. Why wouldn't she answer? She'd obviously been upset about my asking for that release. What if, knowing the jig could be up, she was now stretched out, in some overdosed haze on the floor? Maybe on the kitchen floor with the gas burners going full blast without flames. The more my neurons circled around these unhappy thoughts, the more concerned I became. It would be horrible if she committed suicide after my telephone call.

What would I say at the coroner's inquest when they asked me what I had asked her for on the phone? "Wouldn't it have been better to talk to her in person, Dr. Cline? Wasn't it apparent you were perhaps dealing with a sick person?" Suicide would be sad for Joyce and massively inconvenient for everyone else.

I made a telephone call to The Willows. We obtained Joyce Smith's

63

address. She lived in a housing project complex, up on the third floor. John and I drove to place and found the building wedged in between look-alikes. We took the elevator, and knocked loudly at the door.

There is no answer, so we knock longer and louder. No luck. The shades are drawn at the window. Now I was even more concerned that the gas might be hissing out full blast and Joyce might be stretched out on the kitchen floor.

I will relate the following just as I experienced it.

John and I hustle down to the apartment complex office and I tell the blonde at the desk, "We just gave a lady some rather bad news about two hours ago. Now I'm concerned for her. She doesn't answer her door and we're afraid she may have hurt herself or have committed suicide. We'd like to get in."

This definitely catches the blonde's attention. But surprisingly, in this large complex, she too knows about Joyce and her approaching end of life. "Oh, you're talking about the lady who is dying. Isn't it a shame how sick she's been lately?" The blonde has been told by Joyce that her brother was about to die, too. "Is this bad news about him? Is he still with us?"

"No," I assure her, "the bad news wasn't about one of Joyce's relatives."

Maintenance is phoned. Only maintenance has the legal right to enter the apartment without owner consent. It's a long wait for the man in the blue overalls who finally arrives, keys jingling.

We take the slow-moving elevator up to the third floor and maintenance knocks loudly at the door. No answer. Finally, he raps on the doorknob with his keys and yells "MAINTENANCE" in a voice that would wake the dead. Still no answer. So he starts fumbling to find the right key to put into the keyhole and jams it in. But before he can open it, the door is opened hesitantly from the inside. There stands Joyce.

When she sees me and John Branson, her face pales and she looks stricken. I say lamely, "Hello, Joyce." John Branson and I just walk right in; the maintenance man disappears. The TV is on. Crackers and cookies are on a little table and there are crumbs scattered across the floor.

Joyce has obviously just been sitting there stuffing herself, watching a soap opera and simply not answering the door. Or our calls! How irritating! I told her that we had knocked earlier and there was no answer. She said that she had been in the back bedroom and probably did not hear it over the TV. I think "no way." But what I say is, "Joyce, I just came from the clinic. Where's the written release?"

She says, "I talked to Dr. Knox about that on the phone."

I act really angry. My eyes spark their best spark. Now I say it: "No way! I was just talking with Dr. Knox. I talked to his girls. You didn't phone. The jig is up, Joyce. I've talked to Dr. Knox." I thought it best not to let Joyce know, that at this point, that Dr. Knox wouldn't say much. I'm very careful not to say that Dr. Knox had given information. I just say we had talked. The implication, of course, is that he had spilled the beans.

I go and stand right in front of Joyce Smith, real close, while John Branson looks on with a kind of horrified fascination. I go on with my no-nonsense monologue.

"You're in a situation like an alcoholic, Joyce. Now everything is open. And you can either be straight now or it can go on and get a lot worse for you and a lot worse for the people at The Willows. You need to make some better choices *right now.* There may be time to pull this thing out of the fire if you handle it correctly. If you don't, it's going to be a lot harder on the people there. But most important, it's going to be a lot harder on you." That's the ticket, I'm thinking. Pretty heavy confrontation with a good sprinkle of hope and empathy.

Joyce looks at me blankly and silently. She's very good at that. There's just no way to know what the lady is thinking. John Branson said later that he thought she was going to pop me right in the face. However, I didn't really pick up on that. But she did surprise me a bit by simply saying, "What do you think I should do?"

That's a reasonable question. What should she do? I start thinking, "Let's get this little side show on the road, do a performance and get it over with. If days pass before Joyce tells the facility about her charade, some new manipulation will be dreamed up, or lawyers will be involved, or who knows what."

"Joyce," I say, "you need to go back with me to The Willows now and talk with the people there about the stunt you have pulled. You need to be honest."

She asks, "Do you think they'll ever forgive me?"

"The human heart is a funny thing. They actually might."

In silence Joyce gets her coat and we march out. The three of us. Joyce, I think, must look sort of like a prisoner shuffling along between two guards. John walks first. Joyce is in the center and I bring up the rear. Three quiet people just marching along. We squeeze into John's Volkswagen, Joyce stuffed in the back seat, and we drive the fifteen minutes to the nursing

65

home. The trip is very quiet. John's eyes still register shock at the whole situation. Mine are determined, and Joyce is leaking tears.

On arriving at The Willows, John broadcasts on the PA that there will be a special staff meeting in the dining room. I decide to lock in a bit of honesty from Joyce, so, when she and I are left alone briefly in his office prior to the meeting, I say, "Joyce, I don't want you to say one thing more or less than Dr. Knox would say if he were talking to the staff." Joyce's eyes widen to full moon. The thought of Dr. Knox talking to the staff obviously is a cosmic jolt to her.

"Who is going to be at this meeting?" she asks in a tremulous voice.

"Hopefully everyone you have conned," I answer.

John returns to the office and we all walk down the hall to where about thirty people, more or less, sit in stunned silence.

I start out briskly, "Well, glad everyone's here." I try and keep my voice light. There are some old Christmas decoration boxes laying on the floor and I say, "Well, I guess it's Christmas in February." Just talking. Smile on my face. Keeping it light.

I continue, "Group, Joyce has something to say to everyone. I think all of us have things about ourselves that would be difficult to tell others. Joyce has decided to come here and tell the truth. It's tough. Okay, Joyce, hit it." Joyce looks up at me with a definite questioning "what should I say?" look.

I stare at her with my most forceful look that I hope clearly says, "Don't pull that. Just be straight. Start now." I do say, "What would Dr. Knox be saying?"

The mention of Dr. Knox jumpstarts Joyce. "I have lied to everyone." Then her engine coughs and sputters and she starts dropping tears all over the floor. They are running down her immobile round face. She doesn't appear to really be crying, just flooding out.

Someone shakily asks, "What did you lie about?" Joyce replies, "About my illness. About everything."

People are stunned. No one knows what to say.

Finally, in a quivering voice, someone asks, "*Everything?*"

After a moment, one lady asks, "What about your hair?"

"I cut it off with scissors."

"What about the blue spots on your arms?"

"It was paint."

"What about the high sed (sedimentation, a blood chemistry) rates?"

"I overdosed on aspirin."

The two people who have been practicing their song for Joyce's funeral start crying. A general wailing starts as several others join in that new chorus.

Elaine Erickson, who had helped Joyce pick out a casket says, "Well, I gotta say, I'm angry. I feel like I've been taken!"

Others ask questions along the line of, "Why did you do this, Joyce? Didn't you know we love you? We loved you before you were sick!"

Joyce Smith says she doesn't know why she did it. She says that she just needed friends. She's still dropping tears all over the floor. More people start crying.

The head of housekeeping, Della, one of the women who had been secretly thrilled about the opportunity to sing at the funeral and who had put in hours of practicing, starts crying. She says, "My kids...the families...everybody will be so disappointed...." then she checks herself and says, "We just wanted to make your funeral beautiful for you."

At this point, the people in the room are obviously sorting themselves into the "beyond hacked off and angry group" and the "poor Joyce we have to love her" bunch. One of the floor nurses, a leader in the latter group says, "Well, I've just got to say I'm happy. I'm happy Joyce isn't going to die. I love Joyce." I think this is said to counter the folks who appear really disappointed that the funeral appears to be put on hold.

Several people nod their heads affirmatively, agreeing. The people who were planning to sing at the funeral cry harder. One person gets up and stomps out without saying anything, obviously pissed.

Then the meeting sort of trickles out. The director of nurses tells Joyce that she still has a job if she wants it, but with the requirement that she seek psychiatric care. And Ann notes emphatically, "And I want a weekly report from the doctor about how you are doing."

Joyce nods her head in agreement. There's not much else for her to say. Most of the thirty people have nothing more to say, either. There is still the "stunned" and "this can't have happened" feeling about the place.

Finally, several people start crying harder, get up and run over to hug Joyce, who is sitting there crying harder in response to their hugs and then responds with a hug in return.

The human heart is often not real bright. But it beats with a forgiving throb. Thus, in one afternoon, the whole issue was explained and Joyce was supported and set on her way to recovery.

The next night there was to have been a staff/resident blowout party to celebrate Joyce's supposed remission. The staff decided to still have the party, as residents were expecting it. But now the reason residents were given for the celebration changed. The party wasn't for Joyce's remission, but for the cure that had been miraculously found for her illness!

Made in the USA
Middletown, DE
21 December 2017